Beatrix Farrand's
PLANT BOOK FOR
DUMBARTON OAKS

Beatrix Farrand's
PLANT BOOK FOR
DUMBARTON OAKS

REVISED EDITION

JONATHAN KAVALIER

Editor

New Preface by
THAÏSA WAY

DUMBARTON OAKS, TRUSTEES FOR HARVARD UNIVERSITY
WASHINGTON, DC

© 1980, 1993, 2022 Dumbarton Oaks
Trustees for Harvard University, Washington, DC
All rights reserved.
Printed in China by Martin Book Management

LIBRARY OF CONGRESS CATALOGING-IN-PUBLICATION DATA

NAMES: Farrand, Beatrix, 1872–1959, author. | Way, Thaïsa, 1960– writer of preface. | Kavalier, Jonathan, editor, writer of introduction; writer of added commentary. | Bliss, Mildred, 1879–1969. Attempted evocation of a personality.

TITLE: Beatrix Farrand's plant book for Dumbarton Oaks / new preface by Thaïsa Way ; introduction and commentary by Jonathan Kavalier, editor.

OTHER TITLES: Plant book for Dumbarton Oaks

DESCRIPTION: New edition. | Washington, DC : Dumbarton Oaks, Trustees for Harvard University, [2022]. Includes essay "An attempted evocation of a personality" by Mildred Bliss, reprinted from Beatrix Jones Farrand, 1872–1959: an appreciation of a great landscape gardener (Washington, DC: Mrs. Robert Woods Bliss, 1960).

SUMMARY: "The Plant Book for Dumbarton Oaks was prepared by Beatrix Farrand as a resource for those charged with maintenance of the Dumbarton Oaks Gardens following their acquisition by Harvard University in 1941. To commemorate the 100th anniversary of the gardens, and in conjunction with Farrand's 150th birthday, this new edition contains updated commentary and new contemporary and historical photography, showing the gardens in all their current beauty and as they were conceived and created. Accompanying the original plant lists, Farrand's text carefully explains the reasoning behind her plan for each of the gardens and shares how each should be cared for in order that its basic character should remain intact. While she provides suggestions for alternative plantings, strictures concerning pruning and replacement, and exposition of the overall concept that underlies each detail, Jonathan Kavalier's thoughtful commentary provides context for changes that have affected new plant choices for the gardens, such as new, disease resistant cultivars and recognition that some plants are now considered invasive. This book is an excellent companion to a stroll through the garden for any lover of plants and landscape architecture, and any fan of Farrand's garden design." —Provided by publisher.

IDENTIFIERS: LCCN 2021048038 | ISBN 9780884024811 (paperback)

SUBJECTS: LCSH: Plants, Ornamental–Catalogs and collections–Washington (DC) | Dumbarton Oaks Gardens (Washington, DC)

CLASSIFICATION: LCC SB466.U7 F37 2022 | DDC 635.909753–dc23/eng/20220107

LC RECORD available at https://lccn.loc.gov/2021048038

BOOK DESIGN AND COMPOSITION: Melissa Tandysh

COVER ILLUSTRATIONS: (front cover) Looking through the Fountain Terrace gate toward the Terrior Column. Farrand designed this gate to include representations of Wisteria, Dicentra, and Zantedeschia, echoing plants in the gardens. Photograph by Sandy Kavalier, 2020; (back cover) Rateau-inspired urn and Narcissus 'Thalia' in Camellia Circle. Photograph by Sandy Kavalier, 2020.

FRONT MATTER ILLUSTRATIONS: (i): Lovers' Lane Pool looking north toward Mélisande's Allée. Photograph by Alexandre Tokovinine, 2010; (ii–iii): Looking south toward the Main House and barn that would later become the Green Garden and swimming pool loggia, ca. 1900. LA-GP-25-7, Garden Archives, Dumbarton Oaks, Trustees for Harvard University.

www.doaks.org/publications

Contents

THE PLANT BOOK

THE MUSEUM WING AND AREA NOT GENERALLY OPEN TO THE PUBLIC 229

Beatrix Jones Farrand, ca. 1925. Beatrix Jones Farrand Collection,
Environmental Design Archives, University of California, Berkeley.

An Attempted Evocation of a Personality

MILDRED BLISS

Reprinted from *Beatrix Jones Farrand, 1872–1959: An Appreciation of a Great Landscape Gardener* (Washington, DC: Mrs. Robert Woods Bliss, 1960), 9–17.

IN THE DEATH of Beatrix Farrand the American Society of Landscape Architects has lost the last surviving member of that farsighted and talented group which founded the society and created landscape architectural standards in this country; and the world has lost a most unusual and a rarely gifted woman.

In her girlhood the shrewd intellect of John Cadwalader, her able lawyer-uncle, had already recognized the exceptional abilities of his strong-willed niece. "Let her be a gardener, or, for that matter, anything she wants to be. What she wishes to do will be well done." So he punctuated her British garden trips by giving her shooting parties in Scotland where the gillies pronounced her "As guid as the best shot of a man"; and from her European travels, whence descriptive letters testified to her taste, he pondered her keen powers of observation and her concentrated reading. Finally, having won over the prejudices of late Victorian standards of what became a "lady," Beatrix Jones settled down to work at the Arnold Arboretum under Charles Sprague Sargent.

Never was a great teacher granted a pupil more ideally suited to his hopes. His knowledge was absorbed by her eager young intelligence, and the elderly Professor Sargent saw his dream of the continuity of horticultural research in this country assured. And then one day the pupil submitted the plan of a garden—paths, benches, group plantings in height and color—and the professor frowned. "Don't waste time on what you call design. You must hybridize and propagate. The only paths necessary are merely for accessibility and there is no time to sit on benches; a tree stump will do as well."

Later the pupil made one more effort to stir the comprehension of gardens as an aim in itself, but the master of horticulture could not understand. Sadly, he saw

I

his dream vanish and his beloved pupil leave Jamaica Plain and enter, one might say, her very personal garden gate.

The following years brought Beatrix Jones experience in the making of small and of large gardens; in forestation and in giving design and varied unity to university campuses—Princeton, Yale, and Chicago—and simultaneously her reputation grew. With her marriage to Dr. Max Farrand, the recognized authority on Benjamin Franklin, and their removal to San Marino, Mrs. Farrand adapted her ideas born of the California climate, topography, and plant material to new treatments and painted her living pictures with hitherto untried palettes. Here too, she again proved her especial genius for architectural adaptation by converting a nondescript, four-room cube into an elongated and particularly charming home with dignity and every comfort, well suited to the distinguished director of the Huntington Library and his guests. Her profound love of trees and plants gave her an understanding—one is almost tempted to say psychological understanding—of their idiosyncrasies. But however definite their preferences and her ready obedience to their needs, she managed somehow so to place her axes that the vista she wanted took its place as if by happy accident.

Unfailingly courteous, she used her expressive and beautiful hands competently to explain the work to the mason and the bricklayer; or to demonstrate how and when to prune; or even, when teaching a novice, to lay a few yards of drain herself. She was, in fact, a thoroughly efficient dirt gardener: her knowledge of plant material had never been limited to landscape gardening, nor the designing of a livable house to that of the gazebo. Beatrix Farrand knew all of the problems and ignored none of the difficulties of the exacting but Gentle Art of Gardening.

Always preoccupied with scale and quality in every manifestation of the humanities, her imagination, constantly stimulated by association of ideas, was forever creating enriching surprises for the amateur. The tending of an individual plant, the protecting of a stone or marble unit, the care of a wooded hillside equally touched unsuspected responsiveness in the simplest of her fellow workers. They were proud to be associated with her and enjoyed watching the new horizons she unfolded to them.

While absorbed in making a new garden she kept the individuality of all other gardens untouched by the personality of the new denizen of her prolific imaginary world. She wrote little so as to create the more. Profoundly sensitive to music and with a fine voice, her greatest sacrifice had been abandoning the promising career of a singer when she put herself to work under Professor Sargent. However, she never looked back over her musical shoulder, but transferring her sense of rhythm to the world of nature composed her visual symphonies.

Redeeming the long-neglected but fine estate of Dartington Hall near Totnes in Devon gave Mrs. Farrand especial pleasure. The lay of the land, the climate, the farsighted planned-purposes, and the friendly owners appealed to her, and the results she obtained were noteworthy until World War II arrested her work.

But her two greatest loves were her own inherited property of Reef Point at Bar Harbor on Mount Desert Island and Dumbarton Oaks in Washington, DC. On seven acres bounded by Atlantic rocks and a sweep of sea, she so placed her sheltering conifers and secluded paths that a most astonishing variety of shrubs, flowers, and ground cover became a fascinating enclave of erudition on the scrubby coast of Maine. There she was able to grow plants found as far north as Newfoundland and as far south as North Carolina. This horticulturist's paradise could have been the enlightening lantern to guide the researchers of the future along the road of experimentation—an example of obtaining the greatest use from a small area and of reaping a large harvest from modest means. But among other insurmountable obstacles the difficulty of assuring competent maintenance over years to come loomed too large and Reef Point is no more. Its library, herbarium, and the invaluable collection of Gertrude Jekyll's notes and papers are now properly housed, used, and prized by the University of California in Berkeley.

The gardens at Dumbarton Oaks were perhaps one of the most difficult problems presented to her, for she found not only an existing and a rather dominating house and an unusually wide variety of grades, but also the very definite personal preferences of the owners with their special interest in design and texture. The gardens were to be for spring and autumn enjoyment and in winter were to have perennial green in abundance. A swimming pool, tennis court, and brook completed the illusion of country life, while clever planting bordering the lawn screened the street on the south side and left the birds undisturbed. The onrush of spring at Dumbarton Oaks fairly leaves one breathless before the great billowing mass of forsythia tumbling down two hillsides turned to gold. This and the aerial white hedge of pollarded pear trees are imaginative plantings seen nowhere else.

Such were Mrs. Farrand's integrity and loyalty that, despite the long absences necessitated by the professional nomadism of the owners, never in all the years did she impose a detail of which she was "sure" but which the owners did not "see," and never were the owners so persuasive as to insist on a design which Mrs. Farrand's inner eye could not accept. A deepening friendship born of intellectual challenges, of differing tastes, and of the generous tact of her rich wisdom made the years of their close association a singularly happy and most nourishing experience. Never did Beatrix Farrand impose on the land an arbitrary concept. She "listened" to the light and wind and grade of each area under study. The gardens grew naturally from one another until now, in their luxuriant spring growth, as in the winter when leafless branches show each degree of distance and the naked masonry (from brick and limestone near the house, through brick and gray stone in the rose garden, towards stone only in the fountain terrace, and finally to the stone and wood leading to the apple orchard), there is a special quality of charming restfulness recognized by thousands of yearly visitors.

There is a touch of whimsy here, an arresting breadth of scale there; and yet there are details so unobtrusive that they have to be looked "at" to be seen.

Thus, Dumbarton Oaks has its own personality sculptured from Beatrix Jones's knowledge and wisdom and from the daydreams and vision of the owners. The bonds of friendship and affection were firm and the guiding "anima" of Beatrix Farrand will linger in all the highlights and shadows. One's constant effort will be to make the future of the Dumbarton Oaks gardens worthy of their birthright.

Foreword to the 1980 Edition

DIANE KOSTIAL MCGUIRE

Beatrix farrand's *Plant Book* was written in 1941, in a period of critical importance to the preservation of western culture, so many elements of which are represented at Dumbarton Oaks. During those dark and difficult days, the humanist ideals exemplified in the creation of the Byzantine Library by Robert Woods Bliss and embodied in the imagination of Mildred Bliss, expressed in her creation of the gardens, were threatened with extinction. To some who had been born before the turn of the century, who had experienced the Great War, the dynamic optimism of the twenties, and the economic upheavals and consequent political struggles of the thirties, there was a realization of the magnitude of the threat. The bright lights of European culture and art were soon to be dimmed, and the basis of our civilization was challenged.

Almost forty years later these ideals are still threatened, but we now have come to value our own cultural assets and through the preservation movement are taking an active part in assuring their continuance in the future. The decision to publish the *Plant Book* is a recognition of the premise that the gardens at Dumbarton Oaks form a significant part of our cultural heritage. The gardens are important because they represent a uniquely American adaptation of the classical Mediterranean garden form which traveling Americans came to admire in the late nineteenth century and which was so eloquently described by Edith Wharton in *Italian Villas and Their Gardens*. The design of the plantings follows the tradition of Gertrude Jekyll, with a palette adapted to the rigors of our continental climate and with a selection of tree species predominantly North American.

Beatrix Farrand's *Plant Book* is the cornerstone on which the plan for the preservation of the gardens at Dumbarton Oaks is based. Preservation of garden art must be founded on accurate historical documentation, but specific, detailed planting information often is lacking completely or survives in the most fragmentary form. John S. Thacher, appointed in 1940 the first Director of Dumbarton Oaks, was given the responsibility of overseeing its garden as well as administering its scholarly affairs. It was most important at that time to provide a smooth transition as the estate was turned over to Harvard University by its owners. Realizing that inevitably changes in the gardens would need to be made, that certain functions would be altered or eliminated, and that maintenance standards would be lowered in the future, he requested that Beatrix Farrand, who had been commissioned by Mildred Bliss in 1922 to design the gardens, write a plant book that would become a guide for their future upkeep and development. This was a request which demonstrated remarkable vision on the part of John Thacher, and it resulted in this unique document that describes measures to be taken when plants need replacement, the various levels of maintenance required, the design concept of each part of the gardens, why particular choices were made, and why certain ideas were rejected. In addition, forty-two plant lists are included which give the scientific names of the plants growing in the gardens in 1941. It is clear that the meticulous documentation in her *Plant Book* was an arduous and time-consuming task for Beatrix Farrand who, at almost seventy, had been working on the gardens for twenty years. The very nature of the gardens, their organizational complexity, and her own conscientious nature which caused her to suffer anxiety over delay or inaccuracy, made the compilation of the book a labor of love requiring immense perseverance. But thanks to her dedication, and the foresight of John Thatcher in engaging her for this task, we have a document of great value, not only to Dumbarton Oaks but to the historical record of the development of landscape architecture in twentieth-century America.

It is indicative of Beatrix Farrand's interest in plants as a fundamental part of landscape design that in the course of her long, professional career she always described herself as "Landscape Gardener." She did not adopt the appellation "Landscape Architect" although she was, in 1899, one of the eleven founding members of the American Society of Landscape Architects. An Anglophile, she was in close sympathy with the English gardening movement and was particularly influenced by the planting design of Gertrude Jekyll, as well as by the high standards of garden maintenance in that country. When it was necessary, in 1955, to disband the Reef Point Association, which managed her own gardens in Bar Harbor, Maine, because, among other things, there was little prospect in the future of assuring the high quality of maintenance which she insisted on and felt was an integral part of garden design, she ruefully remarked in her address to the trustees that "it became increasingly clear to those in charge of running the enterprise that the inhabitants of the region do not have horticultural sap running in their veins as is emphatically the case in Britain."

She possessed to a rare degree the qualities which are of the highest value to the landscape gardener: a strong sense of design and a consuming interest in and knowledge of plants. At Reef Point she was able to carry on her horticultural interests through her living collection of rare plants in the gardens as well as in the formation of her herbarium. Her garden library, of great horticultural distinction, was a reference collection of numerous titles which included rare volumes, such as Giovanni Battista Falda's *Le Fontane di Roma* or Gerard's *Herball*, or *General Historie of Plants*, as well as antiquarian books of great practical value, such as Roger Clagg's *Woody Plants for Landscape Planting in Maine* or George Barrell Emerson's *Trees and Shrubs Growing Naturally in the Forests of Massachusetts*. Her formal education in the field of landscape gardening began in the study of plants with Charles Sprague Sargent at the Arnold Arboretum, and she continued her studies throughout her life so that she had an extraordinarily broad knowledge of the plants with which she worked. What distinguished her as a practitioner of the art of landscape gardening was her ability to use plants as strong design elements in themselves, providing form, texture, color, and depth. Her approach is masterful. The identifying characteristics of her work are evident in simple plantings, such as the path to the fields from the director's house at the Huntington Library, and in the complexities of texture and color which form the substance of the design for the east lawn at Dumbarton Oaks.

Beatrix Farrand's planting design is characterized primarily by an apparent simplicity, but on close observation one realizes its extraordinarily subtle and complicated nature. It is worthwhile to analyze her planting in order to gain an understanding of how the parts are put together and synchronized to form the whole. This quality of harmony explains the atmosphere of "restfulness" which one experiences in all her gardens. Restfulness and simplicity are by themselves not enough to distinguish a garden, but when executed with imagination and intelligence, true distinction is evident.

In her planting designs the formalism which characterized most of her work comes through clearly and is the point of departure for each planting scheme. Plants were of primary importance as markers—generally there were two symmetrically placed, but sometimes two or three to one side, which indicated an entry or an important point of transition within a garden. In certain instances her planting design is symmetrical. Where it is, there are sufficient irregularities in the placement of the plants to ensure that there is no sense of monotony. More commonly, her plantings have a well-balanced asymmetry. At Dumbarton Oaks, as one enters each part of the garden, particularly each enclosure, the arrangement is such that one comprehends the whole and then examines the detail. The balanced planting within a space contributes greatly to this sense of completeness, and yet, because of the markers and the arrangement of specimen plants, there is also a sense of progression from one space to another. It is the use of plants in such controlled and subtle ways that distinguishes the work.

A study of the plant lists reveals Beatrix Farrand's strong reliance on the broadleaf evergreens to form the structure of the design and to provide strong textural interest as well. The hollies and boxes do both, and they possess enormous versatility. The extraordinary Box Walk at Dumbarton Oaks is an example of Beatrix Farrand's taking the most common element found in almost every garden in the southern United States and transforming it into an original art form. The ascent of the brick steps through the boxwood is an experience in rhythm and progression comparable to a musical composition. The texture of boxwood, which forms such fine and delicate hedges in her gardens in Washington and at Bar Harbor, was replaced in the California work by *Myrtus communis*, which like the others had the advantage of a Mediterranean tradition.

The history of plant use was of great importance to Mildred Bliss, who wanted not only to live in a "country" estate but to have at the same time the feeling that her garden was old and furnished amply with historic associations. Compared to the intentions of the sixteenth-century Italians who placed antique statuary and broken remains from the classical world in their gardens to remind them of vanished glories, the aim at Dumbarton Oaks was not so intellectual, but more emotional and direct. The three plants most commonly used in the garden, the yew, the holly, and the box, are the embodiment of our deepest associations with the gardens of the Old World and with the cottage gardens of England.

Because of the irregularities of the terrain at Dumbarton Oaks and because there were to be both formal and informal spaces, Beatrix Farrand saw the opportunity to arrange the planting of trees in unusually interesting configurations. When work began on the gardens in 1922, there were on the property many fine existing trees, primarily oaks, some of which she integrated into her garden scheme (some have since died and not been replaced). Silver maples, oaks, Japanese maples, the katsura, and beech were admired by Beatrix Farrand, and she worked many of these trees into her design with success. Of course, during the construction of the gardens others had to be removed because of the extensive amount of grading or because parts of the property had not been brought under cultivation before.

In many instances trees were used in the European manner and it is this characteristic, more than any other, which gives the gardens their distinctively Old World atmosphere. The Kieffer pears at the end of the Herb Garden were planted in the style of the Tuscan gardens of the early Renaissance as a double aerial hedge with "look-outs" that allow the view to be framed in a series of panels. The *Magnolia grandiflora* espaliered against the house is an example of the use of an American tree in the European way. In the manner of Italian orchards, apples, cherries, and crabapples have been planted on the hillsides, more for their effect than for their fruit, although Beatrix Farrand did recommend to John Thacher that the apple orchard become more productive through the planting of good, heavy-bearing varieties.

Adjacent to the Music Room, extending to what was formerly the *boulin-grin*, or bowling green, is the Copse. It retains today only a trace of its original form because of the construction in 1963 of the Pre-Columbian Museum, but its former importance is clearly indicated in the 1935 topographical view of Dumbarton Oaks that is mounted over the Music Room fireplace. This little wood provided a contrast to the open terraces and to the more controlled arrangements of trees in other parts of the property. Though the Copse was the largest naturalistic planting, groups of smaller trees were planted elsewhere in order to convey the atmosphere of woodland in a very small space. The group of *Cornus florida* outside the Fountain Terrace is placed in such a way as to suggest an extensive wood outside the wall and to form a transition between the small, enclosed gardens and the broad, south and east lawns.

Although sculpture is used in the gardens, it is on a modest scale. The specimen trees themselves assume the proportion of monumental sculpture. The large beech on the Beech Terrace, the magnolias adjacent to the Box Terrace, the silver maple reflected in Lovers' Lane Pool are examples of trees skillfully placed to achieve a sculptural effect. They are not incidental to the composition but dominate and form the central focus. Most of the varieties of trees used in this manner have good winter form or bark that gives them year-round interest.

The screen plantings at Dumbarton Oaks are especially distinguished along R Street, where the pattern has altered very little over the years except that a large portion of the understory, which is needed in order to give an illusion of greater depth, has died and has not been replaced because of the lack of light now that the overstory has matured.

There are many progressions in the plantings in the Dumbarton Oaks gardens. It is important to identify and understand these because, when replacements are to be made or changes planned, it is critical that the patterns be uninterrupted. The sequence from Green Garden to Beech Terrace to Box Terrace to Rose Garden is of great importance in the original design. It has been interrupted at a critical point, although for the most part it remains intact and is worthy of examination. One makes one's way from the Green Garden through the Beech Terrace and then toward the axis at the east end of the orangery. The progression is not defined by the classical symbolism represented in many eighteenth-century landscape gardens, such as Stourhead or Castle Howard, but by the elements and characteristics of site, sunlight, color, and texture frequently used for definition in the Italian gardens of the sixteenth century where the plantings themselves define the sequence.

At Dumbarton Oaks this particular sequence begins with the monochromatic use of greens near the house. The brilliant yellow, fall foliage of the wisteria, and the fiery red of the Japanese maple offer a brief seasonal accent. The effect in the Green Garden is especially serene, an effect reinforced by the white flowers of the azalea hedge in the adjacent Star Garden. The wisteria blossoms and the early, white flowers of the *Pieris japonica* are delicate and refreshing and contribute to the coolness that prevails in the north-facing Green Garden where the reflective, glossy leaves of the black oaks produce a shimmering light in this *bosco*.

From these airy heights one progresses to the dense shade and "presence" of the great beech on the Beech Terrace which, because of its broad, low-spreading canopy and closeness to the orangery, gives one the impression of passing through a wood. The stairs to the Box Terrace provide a transition from dense shade to sunlight. Only the smaller section of this terrace, to the south of the walk, represents Beatrix Farrand's own design. On the broader, north side where the stone urn is placed, the sequence has been interrupted by a later design much more fanciful than was originally intended. The south side is relatively somber and severe in its geometry of clipped boxwood and closely cut lawn. The Box Terrace, in its small scale and simple planting, was designed as a kind of "anteroom" before the descent to the color and intricate pattern of the Rose Garden below. The importance of the Box Terrace in the sequence has been considerably diminished by the subsequent elaboration of its ground plane.

The progression from the *bosco* of the Green Garden, north of the orangery, to the Rose Garden is similar in sequence to the descent from the *bosco* to the parterre and water-basins at the sixteenth-century Villa Lante, near Bagnaia, although at Dumbarton Oaks the planting is the central element in the design whereas at Villa Lante the water sequence dominates. An understanding of how the plantings carry out the design at Dumbarton Oaks is essential because the plantings are the most important design element. Because the plants are constantly changing, the design is easily misinterpreted.

The sequence ends in the Rose Garden with a burst of color. The roses provide a consistent warmth and brightness throughout the fine months of the year, as do the plantings in the Fountain Terrace and the Herbaceous Border. Over the years, the clear differentiation of color values between the latter two has been obscured. Originally each of these gardens was designed to display the subtleties and variations of a specific, limited range of color. The Fountain Terrace contained shades of yellow, orange, bronze, and maroon, and the Herbaceous Border, pink, red, lavender, and pale blue. In other parts of the gardens the emphasis was on subtle differences of texture, reflectiveness, and seasonal variation, and these are where the delicacy and sensitivity of Mildred Bliss and Beatrix Farrand are most apparent.

Color is used in some parts of the garden as a wash, in a bold, painterly manner. The best known example is the Forsythia Dell. Perhaps more interestingly, this technique is used on the hillside orchards of cherry, apple, and crabapple, where on the ground the effects of a broad wash are repeated in spring with scilla, daffodils, and a variety of ground covers.

One of the reasons Beatrix Farrand agreed to write the *Plant Book* was that she felt strongly that proper maintenance was critical to the success of her landscape design. She well understood, because of her work at Yale and Princeton Universities, that the standard of maintenance would be very different when responsibility for the gardens was turned over from Mildred Bliss to Harvard University. It is important that we understand the meaning that this had for her as a gardener. Because she was, first and foremost, a "Landscape Gardener" whose primary interest was in the use of plants for their own, intrinsic, design value, rather than in the achievement of a design through a specific, spatial arrangement, she was deeply concerned with the control of plants through continual maintenance. In many of the gardens which she designed in Bar Harbor, she worked directly with the gardeners of the estates over a period of time in order that they should thoroughly understand the design concept and the maintenance procedures necessary to control the plantings in the form and size required by the design.

Foremost in the matter of maintenance was proper pruning. Her direction for maintenance of box in the garden is very much in the Japanese manner—continual clipping in order that the proper relationships of scale be kept. Much of the content of the *Plant Book* is directed to this issue of scale, control, and eventual replacement. Although the standard of garden maintenance in this country was higher in the early years of the twentieth century than it had been, or is likely to be again, the exacting standard which Beatrix Farrand required in the maintenance of her gardens was exceptional even for that time.

Beatrix Farrand's manuscript was not illustrated, as it was intended only for use on the site and she doubtless assumed that her few readers would have ready access to Dumbarton Oaks's rich picture files. In this publication, early photographs depicting stages of planting representative of Beatrix Farrand's concepts have been provided wherever possible. Recent views round out the coverage. Some have been included for comparison with older views, to illustrate changes. Others that stand alone may be compared with the text or with the topographical view mentioned earlier, which is also reproduced and which illustrates the gardens in idealized form.

The topographical view was painted by Ernest Clegg in 1935 in the tradition of the Medici lunettes which were painted at the end of the sixteenth century for the *sala grande* of the Villa Ferdinanda at Artimino. These lunettes showed the extent of the patron's property and suggested the family's influential position in society, its wealth and prestige. Undoubtedly the purpose of this twentieth-century adaptation was the same. It is painted on paper and mounted on a wooden panel above the fireplace in the Music Room. It closely resembles the description of the gardens in the *Plant Book*, and, in addition, it indicates in detail those portions of the gardens, a total of approximately twenty-seven acres, which were not a part of the gift to Harvard in 1941 and are therefore not discussed in the *Plant Book*. The lower portion of the gardens along the stream, which is the entire foreground of the painting, was not given to Harvard University but became part of the National Park system. This section was very likely still cultivated in 1941 and it is unfortunate that we do not have a description of it similar to the descriptions of the gardens in the *Plant Book*. The woodland has now closed in on this section, and vandalism and neglect have taken their toll. However, it is possible to reconstruct the original concept of these naturalistic, spring gardens through field study, general notes about the plantings, and a study of the topographical view. The fate of this part of Beatrix Farrand's work is an illustration of the difficulty of maintaining a "naturalistic garden" in our eastern American wilderness where the slightest neglect will result in the reversion to woodland.

In addition to the photographs and the topographical view, a current map of the gardens, intended as a guide to visitors and as a reference for the text, has been provided. In instances where the names of parts of the garden have changed from the original given in the *Plant Book*, the legend indicates both the names.

The photographs indicate the composition of the plants in their relation to one another. There are also plates which illustrate in detail the characteristics of the plants which Beatrix Farrand used most frequently in the gardens.[1] These engravings are taken from rare books in the Garden Library at Dumbarton Oaks, originally the private collection of Mildred Bliss. Beatrix Farrand, who possessed an excellent library of her own, at Reef Point, on all aspects of horticulture and architectural design related to the practice of garden art, advised Mildred Bliss over a number of years on purchases for the library at Dumbarton Oaks.

Although Beatrix Farrand does not often refer in her *Plant Book* to the Dumbarton Oaks garden sculpture, most of which she designed and had executed by Frederick Coles, it is of enough significance to the art of the garden to include reference to it here. Some of the garden sculpture, such as the antique, limestone, Provençal fountain which was originally in the Copse and which has now been moved to the Ellipse and the eighteenth-century terracotta urn formerly on the Box Terrace, was imported from France by Mildred Bliss. However, the most important sculptures in the gardens are the finials on the gate piers marking the transition from one garden to another. Most of these finials have a floral motif and are carved in stone, although some are a combination of stone and lead or stone and wrought iron. They appear in many of the garden photographs where their importance as markers or accents at points of transition within the design sequence can easily be seen. Pencil-and-ink drawings of a few of these finials appear as ornaments to the text.

A few technical notes on the editing are in order here. Unlike the botanist who invariably identifies a plant by its correct botanical name, or the nurseryman who uses the common or descriptive name, the landscape architect uses a mixed nomenclature which serves two purposes: to properly identify a specific variety of plant in order that there can be no doubt about the reference and, at the same time, to be certain that the reference is clearly understood by the layman who may not have a horticultural background. The text of the *Plant Book* reveals at once that Beatrix Farrand used such mixed nomenclature in her reference to plants. For example, in her discussion of the North Vista she refers to the "*repandens* Yews planted outside the basement windows." In cases where mixed nomenclature occurs it has not been altered. Indeed, we have tried to retain the character of Beatrix Farrand's writing to the greatest extent possible. The original text has been changed only where a sentence simply did not make sense due to a missing word or similar, obvious oversight.

The scientific and common names found in the text are those used by Beatrix Farrand. Where there has been a change of nomenclature since 1941, the new scientific name will be found in the accompanying plant list or in a footnote. Capitalization and other matters of style in respect to Latin and common plant names in the text conform to the practice found in the original manuscript. The guiding concept has been to print the body of the text as if the book had appeared

---

1   While archival photographs allowing for comparisons of contemporary and historic conditions of the garden remain in this volume, the engravings of plants have been removed, as these largely showcased invasive plants which are being replaced with suitable natives in many areas.

in 1941. Only the plant lists and editor's notes reflect current practice respecting botanical nomenclature.

The primary reference guide used in preparing the text was the six-volume 1922 edition of L. H. Bailey's *The Standard Cyclopedia of Horticulture*, a work still unsurpassed in detailed botanical references. In addition, the *Bay State Garden Book for 1938*, the catalog published by the famous Bay State Nurseries in North Abington, Massachusetts, was used as the standard reference for nursery terms and for many common names. In the plant lists, an effort has been made to designate every plant clearly for present-day readers by providing where necessary both old and new scientific names, and common names as well, in order that there may be no mistake about the identity of each plant. The reference for modern nomenclature is *Hortus Third* (New York, 1976). It should be noted by the reader referring from text to plant list that the plant lists include only plants growing in the gardens in 1941. In the lists, the plants are grouped in the order generally found in nursery catalogs: trees, evergreen (needle and broadleaf) and then deciduous; shrubs, evergreen (needle and broadleaf) and deciduous; vines; herbaceous plants; ground covers and bulbs.

The brief entries at the heads of most sections, set in italic, are by the editor, and are primarily to inform the reader of changes in the gardens which have taken place since the original text was written. The eulogy, "An Attempted Evocation of a Personality," was written by Mildred Bliss and privately published in 1960 as part of a memorial volume. As this little book is now out of print, it seemed appropriate to reprint her sensitive and thoughtful essay here, for it gives the reader a clearer understanding of Beatrix Farrand as a personality and reveals the generosity and perceptiveness of Mildred Bliss as well.

The primary impetus and incentive to publish the *Plant Book* has come from Giles Constable, Director of Dumbarton Oaks, who recognized its usefulness in the preparation of a master plan for the preservation, maintenance, and management of the gardens. Elisabeth B. MacDougall, Director of Studies in the History of Landscape Architecture, recognized its value as an historical document and the importance of making it available to a larger number of scholars. We agreed that the book would provide an important text in the teaching of planting design at both graduate and undergraduate levels. Students of landscape architecture often lack a sound grasp of the theory and practice of planting design, largely because the subject is not adequately covered in most schools. Publication of the work of professionals, such as Beatrix Farrand, who are articulate in theory and brilliant in practice will be of immense value to these students.

The major assistance in the editing of the text was provided by Lois Fern, Editorial Associate. Her acute judgment and good sense prevailed in instances of baffling nomenclature. Laura T. E. Byers, Librarian, and her assistant, Marcia L. Hudson, made the Rare Book Room available for the preparation of the manuscript and were helpful in providing illustrations from the Garden Library. Evhy Constable's drawings of sculptural details in the gardens ornament this volume, and she also undertook the search for old photographs. The photographs of the gardens in 1979 and the general photographic work for the *Plant Book* were provided by Ursula Pariser, Photographer for Dumbarton Oaks. Older photographs are from the picture files of Dumbarton Oaks. The map was prepared in 1975 by Doug Graf, Architect. My secretary, Anna Siney, did the typing and attended to many details which helped so much in meeting our publication schedule. Donald E. Smith, Superintendent of Gardens and Grounds, who began his gardening work for Beatrix Farrand at Reef Point, was able to unravel many discrepancies which existed between the descriptions in the text and the gardens as they appear today or even in earlier photographs.

Further afield, Mai K. Arbegast, California Landscape Architect and Horticulturist, responsible for the gardens at Filoli, in Woodside, provided advice on organization, and John C. MacGregor, Horticulturist at the Huntington Library in San Marino sorted out the rose nomenclature. Gary L. Roller, Supervisor of the Living Collections of the Arnold Arboretum, was able to help in the difficult identification of the Prunus family.

I am especially grateful for the assistance of Barbara H. Watson, Landscape Architect, for her detailed notes on the manuscript. In addition, I am particularly indebted to Edward N. Harrington, former Horticulturist at Harvard University, with whom I was fortunate enough to work for a number of years. His working knowledge of maintenance and nursery practice in the 1930s and 1940s has been of great value in the interpretation of the text.

Foreword to the 2022 Edition

THAÏSA WAY

CHARLES SPRAGUE SARGENT is said to have taught Beatrix Farrand, landscape gardener for Dumbarton Oaks, "to make the plan fit the ground, not twist the ground to fit the plan." As a historian who has studied Farrand's work for over two decades, I find that his lesson offers an excellent framework for understanding her designs, specifically those for Dumbarton Oaks, a garden and landscape that she spent over three decades designing, revising, and guiding. Her *Plant Book* offers a window into how she developed a design that would fit the ground. It was not an easy task. Robert and Mildred Bliss had, in fall 1920, purchased a country home in the city, on the northern edge of Georgetown in the District of Columbia that would eventually include fifty-three acres brought together through a series of purchases. It was a landscape framed by two ridges—one to the south, on top of which stood a federal house first built circa 1801; and one to the north, with pastures and a farm, between which was a small stream that flowed east into Rock Creek. The land, dropping over ninety feet to the stream, had likely already been shaped into a series of relatively flat terraces. The woodland that covered much of the property included noteworthy trees with red, black, and white oaks spreading their canopies across the southern face of the house and tulip poplars, silver maples, and beech trees comprising a mature although not virgin woodland. There were the remains of an orchard that had produced apples for eating and cider-making, as well as a likely kitchen garden, a remnant of what had been a working farm. There were specimen trees, such as a katsura and a purple beech, and a rather large collection of boxwood planted by a gardener who evidently thought about aesthetics more than production. There was the Orangery, a delightful greenhouse for tender plants set at the heart of the landscape, just east of the house. And there were scattered flowerbeds and a lily pond, or at least what remained of one. This was not a blank slate, but a complex geological site with ridges, slopes, streams, and valleys that had been used for multiple purposes, from the Indigenous tribes for millennia to a variety of farmers, politicians, and merchants over the previous two centuries.

The landscape more than the house intrigued Robert and Mildred Bliss as they sought to establish a country estate within the District of Colombia, the nation's capital. Within a year of purchasing the home, Mildred Bliss requested the assistance of the well-known landscape gardener Beatrix Farrand (1872–1959) to design a garden and the landscape. Over the next two decades, Farrand and Bliss would collaborate through letters, drawings, and photographs, as well as visits and walks through the new landscape. With Farrand's design guidance and extensive knowledge of plants, Bliss oversaw the development of an elegant garden and landscape for her home, a place to entertain as well as to find solace and inspiration, that would eventually become the foundation for her important collection of rare books, prints, and manuscripts in garden, landscape, and horticultural history and practice.

In 1940, the Blisses, collectors of art and patrons of learning in the humanities, generously gave their home to Harvard University, with the caution "to remember that Dumbarton Oaks is conceived in a new pattern...that it is the home of the Humanities, not a mere aggregation of books and objects of art; that the house itself and the gardens have their educational importance and that all are of humanistic value." The capacity for the landscape to evolve from a private country estate to encompass both an institution for scholarship and a public park under the care of the National Park Service derives, in large part, from Farrand's remarkable design and stewardship over decades. This is evident not only in the landscape but also in the significant collection of materials pertaining to the garden and landscape held in the garden and house archives at Dumbarton Oaks. The *Plant Book* is a critically important contribution to this collection, as it represents the thoughts of the designer, her intentions for the landscape alongside her words of wisdom and musings on the potential future of the garden. It should be noted that Farrand did not set out to write the book that we have before us today. She began it in 1941 as a mere two-page report meant to guide the maintenance of the garden as it was transformed from a private estate to a research center and museum. It quickly became a more extensive "planting record book" to more carefully guide the stewardship of the land and garden. To assist her in creating this important reference, Mildred Bliss turned to Anne Sweeney (1887–1954), who had come to Dumbarton Oaks in February 1937 to assist with clerical duties. Sweeney was put in charge of the Catalogue House displays and the Garden Guide educational tours, with guidance provided by Farrand. Sweeney compiled Farrand's notes on the garden design and maintenance, making drafts for Farrand to review and approve. In 1944, a first draft was shared with superintendent John Thacher, who found the notes of great use. Work continued on the project until at least 1953, when it appears to have been put aside, as neither Farrand nor Sweeney were engaged with the garden, Farrand having retired in 1948. In 1980, Diane Kostial McGuire, then serving as director of Landscape Studies, compiled Farrand and Sweeney's notes, updated the references, and added the botanical illustrations to create the book that we have before us. It is rare that historians and visitors can access such an important document, as too often such thoughts remain in private archives rather than being shared as a guide for future stewards and curious readers.

Evidence for how Farrand's design fitted the ground is plentiful in the *Plant Book*; however, it is equally essential to understand how she subtly shaped the land to realize the vision of a home for the Blisses and, eventually, a home for the humanities. In 1921, Farrand found a country estate landscape that had been significantly modified and shaped in the previous two centuries, with the addition of houses and barns, drives and paths, and farmyards and gardens. Knowing the landscape that Farrand saw as she undertook its design gives us a more fully rounded reading of what she added, changed, and made anew as well as what she retained, strengthened, and heightened.

Humans have inhabited the region we know as Washington, DC, for thousands of years, with the first semi-permanent settlements dated by archaeologists to around 700 CE. Inhabitants hunted, gathered, and fished, using their settlements as seasonal basecamps. Rock Creek has never been navigable, so it is unlikely that major settlements were placed on what became the Dumbarton Oaks property, but the land was likely used for hunting, gathering, fishing, and even quarrying quartzite and soapstone.[1] With the arrival of Europeans in the seventeenth century, the Rock Creek/Dumbarton Oaks area was soon considered open for new settlements.[2] Nevertheless, while the area was settled by Europeans, the character of the landscape that Farrand would steward as an extension of Dumbarton Oaks remained native woodlands along rocky slopes and a stream, not entirely altered from its pre-European character.

In November 1703, the former indentured servant and colonial military leader Ninian Beall patented the land that would eventually become Dumbarton Oaks. His petition was granted by the Maryland Assembly for 795 acres, and Beall called the land the Rock of Dumbarton.[3] The grant describes the land as adjacent to that of Robert Mason, beginning at the mouth of Rock Creek where it met the Potomac and extended north–northwest from there.[4] The Rock of Dumbarton remained in the hands of the Beall family until 1801. The family's extensive

1   Scott Einberger, *A History of Rock Creek Park: Wilderness and Washington, D.C., Landmarks* (Charleston, S.C.: The History Press, 2014), 17–19.

2   James D. Rice, *Nature and History in the Potomac Country: From Hunter-Gatherers to the Age of Jefferson* (Baltimore: Johns Hopkins University Press, 2009), 20–28.

3   Walter Muir Whitehill, *Dumbarton Oaks: The History of a Georgetown House and Garden, 1800–1966* (Cambridge, Mass.: Belknap Press of Harvard University Press, 1967), 3; and Land Grant: The Rock of Dumbarton (2), Maryland Land Office at Annapolis, Liber C.D., folio 121, November 18, 1703, transcription in the Colket and Van der Poel Papers, folder 6, Dumbarton Oaks Archive. The grant was officially in the name of the Lord Proprietor in exchange for annual rents, but later reforms to Maryland's charter would change the holding to a standard property arrangement.

4   Land Grant: The Rock of Dumbarton (1), Maryland Land Office at Annapolis, November 4, 1703, photocopy in Colket and Van der Poel Papers, folder 6, Dumbarton Oaks Archive.

holdings—and likely the land's challenging topography—made it more useful for livestock raising than for agriculture, a use that would extend into the early twentieth century, including on the Clifton farm sited on the north ridge. Ninian Beall's son, George, inherited the land, along with the cattle and hogs, three rental houses, a storehouse for his personal use, and an orchard with cider production.[5]

In summer 1800, the land was sold to William Hammond Dorsey, a local lawyer and significant Maryland landholder.[6] The Dorseys built the house that remains today.[7] There is anecdotal evidence of gardens at this time, including a family friend commenting on Mrs. Dorsey being "busy directing the Gardener, & was going to have peas and potatoes planted immediately" while on a visit.[8] On another visit, she mentioned getting "a couple of Jilly Flowers" as the purpose for her visit, suggesting that carnations were being cultivated on the property.[9] By 1805, the Dorseys had sold the land, its garden, and its buildings to Robert Beverley of Virginia.[10] The Beverleys were another planter family looking to semiurban Georgetown as an opportunity to pursue social and business ventures. They called the property Arcolophos, "Grove on the Hill" in Greek, suggesting the ongoing importance of the trees and woodland. It is believed the Beverleys built the Orangery, which was modeled after one owned by Robert Beverley's brother-in-law.[11] There are references to the gardens and production in letters, but none of these letters fully describe the estate. John C. Calhoun purchased the land in 1822 and lived on

5   Will of Ninian Beall, Maryland State Archives, January 15, 1717, transcription in the Colket and Van der Poel Papers, folder 6, Dumbarton Oaks Archive; Thomas Willing Balch, *The Brooke Family of Whitchurch, Hampshire, England; Together with an Account of Acting-Governor Robert Brooke of Maryland and Colonel Ninian Beall of Maryland and Some of Their Descendants* (Philadelphia: Press of Allen, Lane and Scott, 1899), 28–32; and Whitehill, *Dumbarton Oaks*, 5.

6   Land Indenture between Thomas Beall of George and William H. Dorsey, District of Columbia Land Book, Liber 5, pages 40–403, July 12, 1800, transcription in the Colket and Van der Poel Papers, folder 4, Dumbarton Oaks Archive; Land Indenture between Thomas Beall of George and William H. Dorsey, District of Columbia Land Book, Liber 7, page 250, May 18, 1801, transcription in the Colket and Van der Poel Papers, folder 4, Dumbarton Oaks Archive; and Whitehill, *Dumbarton Oaks*, 11.

7   Whitehill, *Dumbarton Oaks*, 15.

8   Diary entry of March 17, 1800, from Brodeau Thornton, "Diary of Mrs. William Thornton, 1800–1863," *Records of the Columbia Historical Society* 10 (1907): 198–99.

9   Diary entry of October 7, 1800, from Brodeau Thornton, "Diary of Mrs. William Thornton," 118. These two entries are quoted in the Colket and Van der Poel Papers, Dumbarton Oaks Archive.

10   Land Indenture between William H. Dorsey and Robert Beverly, District of Columbia Land Records, M 12, pages 268–69, April 19, 1805, transcription in the Colket and Van der Poel Papers, folder 4, Dumbarton Oaks Archive; and Whitehill, *Dumbarton Oaks*, 18. Beverley is misspelled as "Beverly" in this document.

11   Whitehill, *Dumbarton Oaks*, 19–20. In a letter to the two genealogists studying the property's history, a historian dated the Orangery to ca. 1805–12, based on the architecture. Professor James Grote Van Derpool, letter to Meredith B. Colket, Jr., January 4, 1957, Colket and Van der Poel Papers, folder 5, Dumbarton Oaks Archive. Colonel Edward Lloyd, brother-in-law to Robert Beverley, built an orangery a few years earlier at Wye House in Talbot County, Maryland.

the property while serving as secretary of war and then, in the initial years, as vice president of the United States. Brook Mackall, a native of Georgetown, purchased the estate in 1829, using it as his primary home as he worked locally as a customs officer for the US government.[12] Each of these owners appeared to cultivate portions of the landscape while retaining significant groves of trees.

It was Edward Magruder Linthicum who would establish what can be most clearly described as gardens for the country house and landscape that he purchased in 1846. He came from an established family in Montgomery County, Maryland, and was the owner of a nearby hardware store (at what is today Wisconsin Avenue and M Street).[13] Linthicum demonstrated an interest in trees and plants, as he sold them from a local nursery via a catalog in his hardware store. He eventually named his estate "The Oaks," reflecting the white oak trees on the property that had caught his eye, yet another reference to the site's trees.[14] He soon expanded and updated the main house, the stone wall with an iron fence along R Street (where he may have also had trees planted as part of the streetscape), and the semicircular carriage drive. As early as 1848, he traveled to Philadelphia to find a gardener, and he returned having hired a recently arrived English immigrant, J. H. Small, to design a garden for his home. Small would go on to design other gardens, and he became known as a pioneer in interior and floral arrangements for several neighborhood estates.[15] Under Small and Linthicum, and with a labor force of enslaved individuals, the gardens emerged as a major showpiece. Linthicum probably improved the Orangery, and he was likely to have planted the ficus vine that spread across the interior of the Orangery today.[16] A friend, George A. Gordon, wrote of the "well-filled greenhouse with flower gardens to the east, wooded lawn in front, grove of forest trees on the west

12 Land Indenture between James B. Beverly and James E. Calhon; Land Indenture between J. Edward Calhoun and Brooke Mackall," District of Colombia Land Records WB 28, August 5, 1829, page 68; and Whitehill, *Dumbarton Oaks*, 47–49. Whitehill even questions how Mackall could maintain the property as long as he did (until 1846) on the limited salary of a customs officer.

13 Whitehill, *Dumbarton Oaks*, 49–51; and Meredith B. Colket, Jr., "History of Dumbarton Oaks," 1958, Colket and Van der Poel Papers, folder 8, Dumbarton Oaks Archive. While Whitehill describes Linthicum as typical of "nineteenth-century self-made men," it seems implausible this was the case. Both the Magruder and Linthicum families had been powerful in Maryland since the earliest years of the colony and probably helped put him in business. The inheritance of his wife Mary included the final four enslaved people on the property, casting further suspicion on the idea that he was self-made.

14 Whitehill, *Dumbarton Oaks*, 49.

15 "Some Men of Washington," *American Florist* 25, no. 897 (August 12, 1905): 80; J. G. Fitzpatrick, "Letter to Robert Woods Bliss, Esquire," July 28, 1922, Colket and Van der Poel Papers, folder 6, Dumbarton Oaks Archive; and Colket, Jr., "History of Dumbarton Oaks," 4–5. Colket mentions the greenhouse built sometime before the Civil War (probably under Small) and notes that the gardens became a real showpiece in this period. Fitzpatrick wrote a very brief version of the Small story to Robert Woods Bliss in 1922 without the name of the gardener mentioned. A piece in *American Florist* about the Small family provided the additional data needed.

16 Colket, Jr., "History of Dumbarton Oaks," chapters 4, 6.

and a gently sloping well-sodded hills in the rear, all of which were kept in perfect order." Further, he noted that "The Oaks" was then considered a showplace of the District.[17] A number of the older trees, including the katsura on the East Lawn, may well have been planted under Small's direction and a formal fountain is evident in a photograph from the 1860s or early 1870s. The property was used for light commercial agricultural production in at least part of this period; it was listed as holding $25 worth of farming implements, two horses, and one cow, and it produced twenty bushels of Irish potatoes, ten tons of hay, $25 worth of orchard produce, and $50 worth of "market gardens" (probably fruit, vegetables, and/or herbs).[18]

Henry Fitch Blount and Lucia Eames Blount bought "The Oaks" in 1891, although the configuration of the land had changed significantly and was much reduced from that owned by the Linthicums. The property was then used as a working farm, with flower gardens north of the house leading to a summerhouse. Their gardener was a German-born florist listed in the city atlas as Henry Zollner.[19] Mrs. Blount planted a rather large number of boxwoods that she purchased from nearby property owners before they moved away; the resulting trees supposedly reached "nearly a hundred feet in circumference."[20] Henry Blount died in 1917, and his widow, Lucia, sold the property to Robert and Mildred Bliss in two transactions between 1920 and 1922.[21] It was this complex and much modified landscape that Farrand would work with to create a design that would simultaneously fit the ground and realize the elaborate imagination of the Blisses.

Of these earlier landscapes, the magnificent oaks caught the eye of the Blisses and may well have been a primary reason for purchasing the site—in addition to

17 Whitehill, *Dumbarton Oaks*, 50.

18 Schedule 4—Productions of Agriculture West of the 7th Street Turnpike, Nonpopulation Census Schedules for the District of Columbia, 1850–1870, n.d., Microfilm M1793, page 717, National Archives and Records Administration. The US Agricultural Census has data at the individual property level only for 1850, 1860, and 1870. I found no listings for 1860 and 1870, which could indicate that there was no production, that the property was not properly enumerated, that the the documents were lost, or that production was for the Linthicum household's subsistence instead of commercial sale. According to a Consumer Price Index inflation calculator (officialdata.org), the $75 in agricultural production would equate to almost $2500 in 2020.

19 John Sargent White, *To Keep the Declaration*, privately printed 1978; and Dead in the Lily Pond, Demented Woman Returns to Old Home to Die, undated from the Blount file, Dumbarton Oaks Archives (in Maureen De Lay Joseph, Kay Fanning, and Mark Davison, *Cultural Landscape Report: Dumbarton Oaks Park, Rock Creek Park*, pt. 1, *Site History, Existing Conditions, and Analysis and Evaluation* (Washington, DC: Cultural Landscape Program, 2000), endnote 12, page 11.28.

20 Whitehill, *Dumbarton Oaks*, 57.

21 Deed Lucia E. Blount to Robert Woods Bliss, District of Columbia Land Records, Liber 4431, page 377, October 15, 1920, transcription in the Colket and Van der Poel Papers, folder 4, Dumbarton Oaks Archive; and Whitehill, *Dumbarton Oaks*, 57. I have been unable to locate a copy of the second deed. In 1920, the census has Lucia Blount still living as the head of a household that included a black female servant and a white male lodger.

its ideal location as a country estate within easy reach of the center of Washington, DC. The views of woodlands to the north would have added to that delight, as would the presence of large trees that enclosed the land on all sides, a feature that Farrand would retain. The Blisses imagined their new home as an elegant landscape with a house, rather than as a grand house with a simple landscape.

Farrand designed a garden and landscape that would, within a decade, exemplify the possibilities of a truly American landscape, drawing on the natural topography, hydrology, and vegetation as well as the improvements by previous owners and gardeners, including the trees that had matured over the previous century. Her design would reflect the elegance of European, particularly French and Italian, garden design that both Farrand and Bliss so admired. This is evident in the design of the garden rooms as well as the elegant garden gates, finials, and ornamental patterns of the pathways. Furthermore, Farrand's deep knowledge of plants and horticultural practices, reflected in her plant lists as well as by her selection of botanical prints for the Garden Library, contributed to character of the garden and landscape, tying it to the region and the world through an intricate merging of native and introduced plants. What transpired was truly a remarkable American landscape and garden that is considered one of the most beautiful gardens in the world (*National Geographic*) and that serves as a significant collection as an extension of the Garden Library and Rare Books Room at Dumbarton Oaks.

How did this topographically challenging landscape with its significant trees and a scattering of structures become the elegant garden that we know today? The *Plant Book* reveals much of Farrand's intentions and thinking as a designer, thus serving as a remarkable asset to the current stewards and to historians, scholars, and designers. Through a close reading of the text and its historical images, one is able to more fully understand how Farrand grounded her design in the nature of the site, with terraces that fit into the slopes, generous stairways that elegantly descend and ascend through the garden rooms, and water features that evoke the stream at the bottom of the landscape and, more broadly, the creeks and rivers of the region.

Farrand's approach in the *Plant Book* is evident in her description of the south front, where she begins by explaining how to ensure that the house, a major architectural entity in the land, is brought into scale with the landscape through plantings of buxus, yew, and holly, all small-leafed plants. Her discussion moves to the South Lawn, where she guides the replacement of the original grand oak trees while paying attention to the need for privacy that was crucial to the Blisses. The section between the house and R Street is meant to retain the character of lawn and broad tree canopies that originally attracted the Blisses. As she moves the reader through the garden, Farrand designates the Green Garden as a quiet terrace built on an existing flat landscape that is well-proportioned to the Orangery on its southern edge. Originally, two oak trees dominated the lawn, echoing the large trees that enclose the estate in every direction. The design of the terrace is formal but in a simple vocabulary without the forced character of symmetry, in keeping with the character of the trees. The Beech Terrace is an extension of this attention to existing trees, as she created a platform around the beech tree in which elegant benches were placed for quiet pleasure. The east wall was positioned so as to retain appropriate drainage and enough room for the root system to thrive. Thus, it was the beech tree as a whole that determined the proportion of the garden room. Farrand's stewardship of the trees—her commitment to retaining them—reveals an extraordinary attention to the existing elements on the ground.

Farrand also inscribed moments of formality as one moves through the landscape. This is most evident as one enters the Main House and immediately faces the North Vista, a long linear lawn framed by trees and ending in a stone wall laced with wisteria, creating a focused view of the woodland to the north, with its towering tulip poplars. A smaller grove of trees, more in scale with the house, was originally sited on the western edge of the property, where the Pre-Columbian Gallery is now positioned. The Copse, as she called it, not only buffered the garden from the street beyond but echoed the woodlands that surrounded the estate with a subtle insertion of ornaments and benches to suggest a human inscription in the woods. Farrand's delight in the woods and trees as they embower the estate is everywhere evident.

Nevertheless, Farrand was not limited to merely refining what she found. She inscribed into the landscape the vision of her clients as well as her own rich repertoire of garden designs from around the world. This is seen in her blending of formal European approaches to garden design with a singularly American pleasure in the wilderness and natural landscapes. Gracious steps descend to the Rose Garden, where the formality of the design is countered by sweeps of color in the tradition of Gertrude Jekyll. This flight of stairs is one of the most elegant ways that Farrand addressed the descent of over forty-five feet from the Orangery to Lovers' Lane Pool. This drop controls the design of the terraces and adjoining stairs so that all would "fit the surrounding natural levels, both to the north and south of these terraces, as nearly as possible, so that the big trees on either side would not be destroyed in carrying out the garden design." Furthermore, the stairs were determined to have six-inch risers with a fourteen-inch (or wider) tread, so that there would be no "weariness in step-climbing" that might detract from the pleasure of the garden. Beeches, oaks, maples, and magnolias tower just outside the walls, both enclosing the garden rooms and framing views afar.

Moving through the formal Fountain Garden, one finds the fragrant Arbor Terrace with its Du Cerceau–inspired arbor covered in wisteria for springtime wonder. Lovers' Lane Pool, Mélisande's Allée, and the Herbaceous Border reveal a rhythmic alteration of formal and informal, designed and natural elements and materials that lead one farther down the slope. Here again, Farrand drew on an existing cow pond that had once served as a lily pond, then repeated an existing row of silver maples to create an allée of arching canopies. The Goat Trail follows the contours of the land with seating tucked into niches. The Cutting Garden, filled with tulips, peonies, and irises, and the Kitchen Garden, with its herbs and vegetables, are sited where there was once a tenant's farmhouse and garden, and thus where the land was already flat and likely revealed good soil. In each of these garden rooms, Farrand fits her design to the ground, and yet simultaneously crafts the land to create a coherent garden within a larger landscape.

The Ellipse was also sited on an existing platform or terrace, and even in it is changed materials today, reflecting a design by Alden Hopkins in 1959, it is a formal moment that is equally an open glade in the woodland. The original fountain, which recalled Villa Lante's woodland fountains, suggests that one is moving ever closer to the natural stream below. Farrand's subtle use of water is played out in the reflecting pool and in a series of fountains that originally revealed more formality near the house and less formality as one moved into the woodland.

Crabapple Hill and Cherry Hill, alongside the Forsythia Dell, offer swaths of seasonal color, the latter sitting halfway down the slope toward the stream and the former sitting just below the swimming pool, a significant part of the formal garden rooms. These groves evoke the earlier orchards as well as the native trees in the woodland across the stream. Beyond in the park is the landscape of woodland and meadow that Farrand and Bliss imagined as an extension of the garden, the landscape as a holder for the garden. While the *Plant Book* does not discuss the park, Farrand's approach to design and stewardship would hold true.

Finally, it is important to note the inclusion of historical and contemporary photographs in the *Plant Book* in order to reveal the remarkable preservation of the original design and to show changes as the plants matured. As the garden became more popular, some changes were made to assure appropriate resilience and care over the long term. These changes are considered in the essay by Jonathan Kavalier, the director of the Gardens and Grounds. Additionally, the book contains a selection of prints from the Rare Books Collection that serve a critical role in linking the garden to the library and museum collections. Farrand, among others, guided Mildred Bliss in her extensive collection of books and manuscripts on garden and landscape history as well as on horticultural and landscape architectural practice. These books represent an essential resource for designers and garden stewards, particularly those working in a historic garden such as Dumbarton Oaks. When the Blisses endowed the garden fellowships, their intention was that young designers and scholars would draw inspiration and wisdom equally from the garden and the library. The *Plant Book* offers lists of the plants used in the garden while also reminding the reader of the collective importance of the garden as a work of art and the library as a collection of books and documents.

Today, the Dumbarton Oaks garden and landscape is a remarkable treasure for its beautiful display of the colors of the seasons in its wisteria, lilacs, cherry blossoms, forsythia, and tulips. Its exquisite ornaments, as seen in the finials, gates, and walls that extend from the house to the bridges along the stream, are works of craft and art. And it is equally significant for its contributions to design, as Farrand remains one of the most important designers of the profession in the early twentieth century. The designed landscape today is a model of how to fit the composition to the ground and expresses the imagination of both client and designer. Each year, as new fellows in the Garden and Landscape Studies program spend a year in residence, they are moved by the power of this very special garden as a work of art and design.

Introduction

JONATHAN KAVALIER

LANDSCAPE ARCHITECT LAURIE OLIN once told me, as we strolled through the gardens, that as designers we must consider time as a medium. I was surprised, not by the reference to time, which I knew was important, but that by the suggestion that as a horticulturist and gardener I was also a designer. Thinking about his words, I was taken by both the idea of gardening as designing and the role of time as a design tool. I have come back to those words repeatedly, and they resonate ever more with each stroll through the gardens at Dumbarton Oaks. I have gained a deep appreciation for how we must use time, which works both for and against us, as we attempt to preserve Beatrix Farrand's masterpiece at Dumbarton Oaks. And I have come to realize how our work as gardeners shapes the design of the garden, in time.

The maintenance of significant historic gardens is a challenging endeavor. As the Dumbarton Oaks Gardens enters their centennial, we must tackle the impacts of invasive plants, diseases, pests, and climate change. There are the challenges of preserving mature trees and their successors that present ever-changing hurdles to the preservation and stewardship of Farrand's genius. There are changes in available cultivars that we must contend with as we sustain Farrand's plant selections. And, since 1940, we have had to consider the ways that public access impacts the garden, sometimes intentionally and sometime unintentionally.

Garden preservationist and landscape architect Peter Hornbeck offered a productive framework for considering maintenance challenges in a historic garden in "The Garden as Fine Art: Its Maintenance and Preservation," which was first presented at a colloquium on the history of landscape architecture at Dumbarton Oaks in 1982.[1] Focusing on maintenance technique and principle, Professor

---

1 Peter L. Hornbeck, "The Garden as Fine Art: Its Maintenance and Preservation," in *Beatrix Jones Farrand: Fifty Years of American Landscape Architecture*, ed. Diane Kostial McGuire and Lois Fern (Washington, DC: Dumbarton Oaks, Trustees for Harvard University, 1980).

Hornbeck sought to guide how gardeners might navigate design intentions and good garden stewardship, specifically in historic gardens and landscapes. He encouraged gardeners (and readers) to consider the designer's priorities regarding scale, texture, color, technique, and plant succession. At Dumbarton Oaks, these principles guide maintenance decisions and provide a framework through which to view challenges and implement solutions.

Such challenges might have been insurmountable, except that we are privileged to have access to arguably the richest collection of documentation for any of Beatrix Farrand's gardens, housed and protected in the Dumbarton Oaks Garden Archives. Correspondence between Farrand and Mildred Bliss reveals the iterative process of the design as it was completed while the Blisses were stationed abroad. Letters, drawings, mock-ups, and photographs demonstrate the depth of discussions that contributed to the final design. Farrand's *Plant Book* is perhaps the most valuable asset in the archives, a preservation bible of sorts. It includes first-person descriptions of intent and imagined maintenance, and it provides invaluable perspectives into her creative thinking and Mildred Bliss's vision for the gardens. These resources also provide valuable documentation that facilitates the conservation and preservation of the garden's vast collection of architectural elements and furniture designed by Farrand, much of which needs extensive intervention after a century of loving use.

In fact, the garden ornament has become a central focus for future strategic garden preservation efforts. A comprehensive survey of nearly 250 pieces was conducted in 2019, allowing for thorough analysis and prioritization. Over the next decade, we plan to undertake systematic conservation work of Farrand-designed ornament, furniture, and architectural elements, such as arbors and trellises. Three-dimensional computer models of the dozens of unique pieces of furniture created by Farrand were also created in 2019 using archival drawings and contemporary field measurements, in some cases making unseen improvements to joinery. These models will now be used for reproduction purposes, negating the need to send one-of-a-kind historic pieces offsite.

Although change is always occurring in the garden, whether through the seasonal growth of plants or the carefully planned maintenance and restoration work, Dumbarton Oaks remains among the most well preserved of Farrand's surviving gardens. Particular rose cultivars may come and go, as pest pressures wax and wane, but the wash of color described by Farrand in these pages remains. New chrysanthemum cultivars on Fountain Terrace and the Herbaceous Border mix harmoniously with heirloom varieties lovingly propagated each year from ancient stock. Tulips will always trumpet the arrival of spring in these garden rooms, and vast plantings of boxwood and forsythia will remain, even as they require considerable time and effort to maintain.

While Professor Hornbeck thoroughly considers maintenance challenges in the context of preserving the designer's intent through scale, texture, and color, we include additional criteria derived from modern horticultural science and practice when making maintenance and design decisions. An important framework for our stewardship is the care and nurturing of a healthy environment and ecological habitat throughout the gardens and landscape, a goal that we believe Farrand would support. We strive to leverage the gardens' ecosystem services—benefits imparted to animals, such as food and habitat—by protecting diverse habitats and increasing horticultural diversity, which, in turn, assist our efforts to reduce chemical inputs. By focusing on strategic succession planning and long-term tree health, perhaps the best example of using time as a medium, we ensure that the structure of the garden will remain even as particular species may prove untenable with changing climates. By conducting quantitative and qualitative soil analysis and improvement, we increase diversity in the soil microbiome, thereby leveraging natural defenses and nutrient cycling. And by tightly managing, removing, and replacing invasive plants, we foster the increase of diversity and promote the ecological health of this cherished place.

Following Hornbeck, there are two main principles that guide our decisions and techniques on a daily and long-term basis. The first, that maintenance practices should conserve the compositional balance in overall arrangement, is widely adopted by the gardeners at Dumbarton Oaks. This might mean retaining the dense rows of boxwood and the brick path of Box Walk or replacing an aging oak tree on the front lawn, as each detail in the design contributes to the composition of the whole. Pruning decisions are often based on the desired scale and proportion of the plantings. This is true for the annual rejuvenation pruning undertaken by gardeners in Forsythia Dell during the slower winter months. This pruning aims to retain the juvenile weeping form of this massing, allowing the arching branches to cascade down the steep hillside. This effect was of central importance to Farrand, and the architecture of this mass planting takes priority over its floral display. Therefore, the forsythia is pruned in the winter when there is adequate time, thereby allowing the gardeners to use more time-consuming hand-pruning techniques across an acre of forsythia. While conventional horticultural practice calls for a post-bloom pruning, our prioritization of plant form dictates the timing, even though this means sacrificing some spring blooms.

A challenge to our approach arises as the garden matures, in particular, when the older trees age and again when they begin to decline. Throughout the *Plant Book*, Farrand references the need to keep trees "constantly replaced" and "trained and pruned," so that they "not be allowed to become too large," suggesting more frequent tree replacements to maintain desired scale, especially in the more formal sections of the garden near the house. It is quite reasonable that trees in formal spaces were periodically replaced to maintain the desired proportions among the plantings in Farrand's time, considering the more abundant labor—in the 1930s, the gardening staff numbered at least thirty-seven rather than the thirteen at present—and the mission to create and maintain a private pleasure garden. Tree removals were likely less controversial in Farrand's time than today, due to a better contemporary understanding of issues such as carbon sequestration and ecosystem services. With the transition of the property from private residence to institutional campus, and with associated changes to simplify maintenance and reinforce garden infrastructure, the goal of tree maintenance shifted to a more preservation-centric approach, whereby trees are retained wherever possible and understory plantings are reimagined when light and soil conditions inevitably change as the trees mature.

In overcoming the possible conflicts of design intent and contemporary stewardship, we manage our trees as a living collection, closely monitoring their health and intervening to encourage good structure and form, just as Farrand did with the significant oaks, beech, magnolia, and katsura trees that she found in the landscape and that inspired her designs for much of the estate. We are inspired by Mildred Bliss's declaration, engraved in stone on the museum wall, "that trees are noble elements to be protected by successive generations and are not to be neglected or lightly destroyed." In many cases, successors for iconic trees in the gardens are selected and planted before their predecessors fully decline. This is necessary due to the many challenges surrounding access to the gardens due to the topography and narrow gates and to the desire to maintain trees that convey the appropriate massing necessary to support the design.

Hornbeck's second principle, that replacements follow the character of the design and/or what remains from the original design, what might be called precedent, offer an important cornerstone of our maintenance strategy. It is essential to understand design intent and precedent before considering plant replacements, especially in a historic garden such as Dumbarton Oaks that was iteratively designed over decades. In this way, we look at intention and at what was actually planted, and we consider how the two perspectives are often in dialogue with one another. Here, we are very fortunate to benefit from Farrand's insight and articulation offered in the *Plant Book*. Throughout the book, Farrand suggests her design intentions and offers suggestions for alternative species, as she was aware of the changing nature of gardens, soils, and growing conditions. These passages allow the reader to more fully understand Farrand's goals and to view the plants as a means of achieving her aspirations. In fact, this sentiment is perfectly captured in a letter from Farrand to Dumbarton Oaks's first director, John Thacher in 1946, written as the *Plant Book* was in development. Farrand envisioned the book "as a whole will be useful more to show the 'temperament' of the place than the actual position of each tree and shrub. When Bryce [the second institutional garden superintendent] said that he wanted the book so that he could abide by it, it made my blood run cold as nothing will so quickly kill the spirit of any place than to have planting slavishly repeated in certain places because it was originally put there." As replacement decisions arise, we look first to Farrand's writings, then to the garden, and finally we broaden our criteria to consider disease, pest resistance, invasive status, and climatic concerns.

Two examples help illustrate these points, the first dealing with changing growing conditions and the second pertaining to the challenges of invasive diseases. The slope from the Star Garden down to Crabapple Hill offers an example of how we have had to modify plant selection due to changes in the garden as it matured. Farrand specified *Rhododendron mucronatum*, a lovely white flowered azalea still present in the Star Garden. When Farrand designed the area, she incorporated a line of weeping willow along the northern end of the swimming pool. The willows and surrounding trees provided deep shade for the whole swimming pool area, thus allowing the azalea to thrive. Sadly, the willows were lost many years ago because of *Armillaria* fungus. It is uncertain that we can replace the willows, as the fungus remains in the soil for long periods of time. With the slope now in full sun, the decision was made to replace the river of white azaleas with the stunning white "Katharina Zeimet" roses, thereby carrying the design in form and color while utilizing different plants growing in drastically different light conditions. If the willows can be successfully grown (and thus can shade the rose bed), then the roses could be replaced by azaleas propagated from the original variety.

For the second example, we turn to Box Walk. Here, we are using every tool at our disposal to battle boxwood blight (*Calonectria pseudonaviculata*), a devastating disease brought to the United States via Europe in the early 2000s and discovered at Dumbarton Oaks in fall 2018. This disease affects all plants in the boxwood family, is most concerning for English and American boxwood, and can persist in the soil for years. Given the prevalence of historic English and American boxwood in the gardens at Dumbarton Oaks, we have taken great measures to ensure that one of Farrand's favorite plants remains well into the future. At the same time, realizing that this biological war can only be won through improved genetics, we have trialed several blight-resistant cultivars in an attempt to eventually replace the English and American boxwood with more resistant cultivars that still have the desired scale and form. While we are confident that we will be able to maintain boxwood (albeit a different species) in the gardens, it is comforting to see Farrand's considerations for its eventual replacement. When discussing Box Walk, she writes: "If, in time to come, the old Box becomes so broken and shabby that it no longer has sufficient beauty to warrant keeping it, it must be replaced by another lovely plant of fine foliage. Nothing will ever be quite as beautiful as the rumpled masses of the Box as they follow the slop of the hill, but this walk mut be kept bordered by some charming plant as this part of the garden design is an integral one and must not be done away with."

Finally, the removal of invasive plants is one of the most challenging interventions that can be realized in the gardens, and one that may seem constrained in the general context of garden preservation. While many historic gardens pledge to preserve what would appear to be a static landscape, often based on incomplete documentation, the challenge of understanding the designer's intent can paralyze action. We are so fortunate to have a deep understanding of Beatrix Farrand's vision, with supporting documentation and rich detailed descriptions. Only through this understanding can we be confident in our work to update Farrand's plant palette to include fewer invasives and instead to incorporate hardier, more ecologically appropriate plants.

Work has already begun on a multi-year, phased effort to replace invasive species, both planted and indicated in designs by Beatrix Farrand, as well as those that have shown up uninvited. This work will not only reduce garden maintenance in the long term but also raise the level of ecosystem services of the entire landscape. The project encourages the growth of plants that have evolved closely alongside native fauna and are thereby better prepared to exist symbiotically. As Doug Tallamy expresses in *Bringing Nature Home*, native plants (particularly woody plants) provide exponentially more benefit for native insects because their lifecycle events, such as flowering and fruiting, are naturally timed with the emergence of these insects.[2] Fruit, pollen, and nectar from these plants are more nutritious for these insects, owing to the fact that the plants and insects have evolved in the same ecosystems for millennia. Such evolutionary symbiosis helps reduce the reliance on chemical interventions including insecticides and fungicides, which, in turn, fosters a healthier soil microbiome, increasing nutrient cycling and other factors that aid in overall plant health. In 2020, we began to introduce compost teas as another way to increase soil health and thus to encourage healthier, stronger, and more resilient plants.

As stewards and gardeners, we carefully weigh each plant's importance in the garden from a design perspective. Virginia creeper (*Parthenocissus quiquefolia*) has its place if carefully managed—as, for example, on the front of the Fellowship House. However, in Washington, DC, wisteria is an invasive plant that spreads vegetatively with an incredible rate of growth and reseeds readily. Because wisteria is of central importance in many of Farrand's designs, we have retained it in those places where it is core to the design, but we are vigilant in removing it from unwanted locations and pruning off seedpods before they ripen. Meanwhile, privet (*Ligustrum* sp.), a shrub that has spread throughout much of Mélisande's Allée—propagating rampantly by seed—is not a central component in any Farrand designs. We can easily replace it with a native shrub such as buttonbush (*Cephalanthus occidentalis*) or arrowwood viburnum (*Viburnum dentatum*), both of which have similar form, bloom time, and color, thus echoing Farrand's design intent.

We are inspired by the garden at Dumbarton Oaks and, like Hornbeck, we consider the garden as fine art, through the artistic lens of scale, proportion, and color. These compositional tools are, indeed, the heart of Farrand's genius. But the garden at Dumbarton Oaks is more than an aesthetic composition, it is a living work of art that must be also cared for as an ecological composition. Farrand's genius in blending intimate, layered spaces across topographically challenging terrain creates highly desirable and diverse habitats for beneficial insects, vertebrates, and other inhabitants. These integral contributors to the garden provide ecosystem services in the form of predation, pollination, and nutrient cycling. Perhaps equally as important, they facilitate use of the garden as a living laboratory to explore ecology and biology, in addition to its more familiar use as a case study for garden design and history.

We must consider all the contributions that the masterpiece of Dumbarton Oaks offers, from beauty and inspiration to carbon sequestration and habitat for native flora and fauna. Especially in this Anthropocene era, we strive to prioritize

---

2 Douglass W. Tallamy, *Bringing Nature Home: How You Can Sustain Wildlife with Native Plants* (Portland: Timber Press, 2009).

ecological responsibility, particularly when considering our duty to maintain sixteen acres of contiguous green space in the heart of Washington, DC. These goals can be integrated with historic stewardship to preserve Farrand's design while also offering continued relevance in the modern horticultural and garden context. I think Farrand, a vocal proponent of native plants, would approve. And armed with a contemporary knowledge of horticultural science and the bountiful plant varieties available to the modern designer, she would no doubt be a vocal proponent for the ecosystem services rendered nearly one hundred years after she began her work.

It is often said that gardening is the slowest of the performing arts. But it is the garden, not the gardener, that holds the lead role, constantly growing, senescing, undulating through plant and soil migration. In this metaphor, I try to act as the producer, setting a long-term vision for an ever-changing and growing place that will continue to contribute to the larger gardening world. The gardeners are the production designers, coaxing the best performance from the plants and carefully shaping their exuberance when needed. Farrand's *Plant Book* is our script and call sheet, and my copy is dog-eared and full of annotations. This book is meant to be used in the gardens, not kept in pristine condition on a bookshelf. And if well used, this book and accompanying garden documentation can help answer the central question always in our minds as we preserve the gardens: what would Farrand do?

Garden and Grounds staff, socially distanced during COVID-19, April 2021. From left to right: (*back*) Rigo Castellon, Donnie Mehlman, Walter Howell, Robby Adams, Marc Vedder, Melissa Brizer, Austin Ankers, and Martin Nji; (*front*) Luis Marmol, Ricardo Aguilar, Kim Frietze, and Jonathan Kavalier. Photograph by Sandy Kavalier.

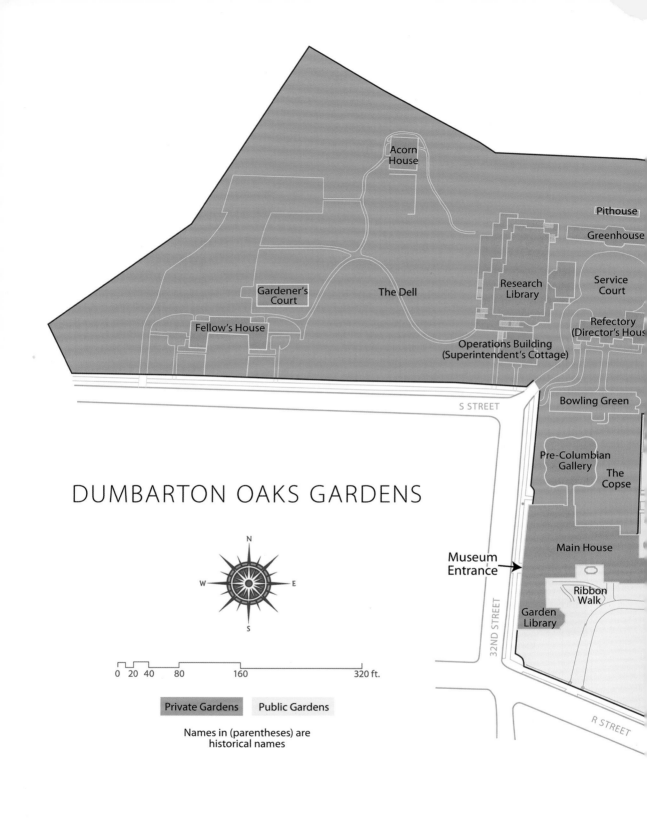

DUMBARTON OAKS GARDENS

Acorn House

Pithouse

Greenhouse

Research Library

Service Court

Gardener's Court

The Dell

Refectory (Director's House)

Fellow's House

Operations Building (Superintendent's Cottage)

S STREET

Bowling Green

Pre-Columbian Gallery

The Copse

Main House

Museum Entrance →

Ribbon Walk

Garden Library

32ND STREET

R STREET

N
W — E
S

| 0 | 20 | 40 | 80 | 160 | 320 ft. |

Private Gardens   Public Gardens

Names in (parentheses) are
historical names

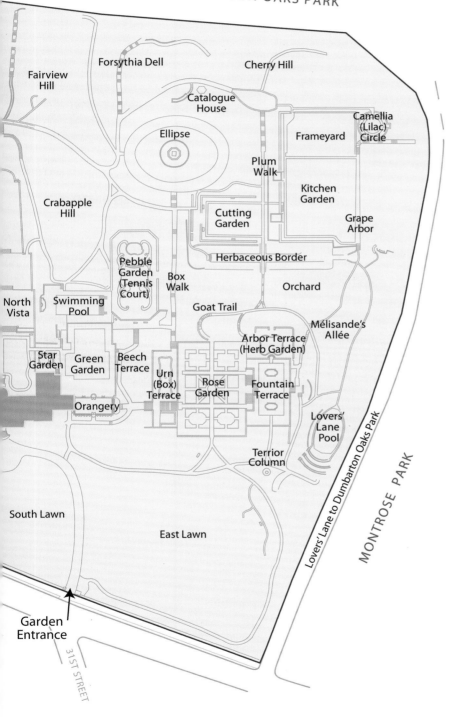

DUMBARTON OAKS PARK

Fairview Hill

Forsythia Dell

Cherry Hill

Catalogue House

Ellipse

Camellia (Lilac) Circle

Frameyard

Plum Walk

Kitchen Garden

Crabapple Hill

Cutting Garden

Grape Arbor

Herbaceous Border

Pebble Garden (Tennis Court)

Box Walk

Orchard

North Vista

Swimming Pool

Goat Trail

Mélisande's Allée

Arbor Terrace (Herb Garden)

Star Garden

Green Garden

Beech Terrace

Urn (Box) Terrace

Rose Garden

Fountain Terrace

Orangery

Lovers' Lane Pool

Terrior Column

Lovers' Lane to Dumbarton Oaks Park

MONTROSE PARK

South Lawn

East Lawn

Garden Entrance

31ST STREET

Looking northeast from the Ellipse toward Cherry Hill, 1944–45. LA-GP-9-4, Garden Archives, Dumbarton Oaks, Trustees for Harvard University.

THE

PLANT

BOOK

THE SOUTH FRONT

Planting around the South Side of Dumbarton Oaks House

The plant varieties in this section of the landscape remain largely unchanged from Farrand's earliest design. The now mature boxwood, abelia, and viburnum are hand-pruned to maintain proper scale in relation to the house, and accents such as winter jasmine and wisteria grace the front steps, mirroring similar plantings in front of the Garden Library. Ivy and porcelain vine (*Ampelopsis brevipedunculata*) were removed from the house walls long ago and have not been allowed to reestablish, as they are known to damage masonry. As the garden matures, we have focused on replacing plants that are today considered invasive, with native or noninvasive plants that support Farrand's design intent and provide better habitat. —JK

THE PLANTING ON THE SOUTH SIDE OF THE HOUSE HAS BEEN CHOSEN FROM material with foliage of small scale in order to give apparent size and importance to the building. Large as the building is, a study of its scale will show the detail as a whole is small. As a general principle, approximately one-third of the spring line of the building should be unplanted, as the effect is unfortunate where a building seems to be totally submerged beneath a line of plants which muffle the architectural lines and make the building appear to rise from a mass of shrubs rather than from the ground.

The first-floor level is high above the ground and it is therefore necessary to screen the unattractive but useful basement windows with plants which mask the lower windows without interfering unduly with light, since the basement rooms are used by working units.

South front of the Main House, 1979. LA-GP-25-82, Garden Archives, Dumbarton Oaks, Trustees for Harvard University.

View from the South Lawn toward the Main House, 2001. Photograph by Joe Mills.

On each side of the main entrance large marker plants are needed. If the small-leaved *Buxus* proves impossible to maintain, Yew, Holly, or *Crataegus pyracantha* (*Pyracantha coccinea*) may be used. No large-leaved plants like Magnolias or Rhododendrons would be fitting, as the effect would be coarse and clumsy. If disease or insect infestation in one kind of plant makes its use unwise, variety may still be maintained by using others selected from the fine-leaved evergreens such as *Ilex crenata*, *Buxus suffruticosa* and *sempervirens*, *Ilex opaca* or *Aquifolium*, *Taxus cuspidata* or *Torreya nucifera*. Conifers such as *Thuja*, dwarf Spruces and Junipers, or *Chamaecyparis* are not thought desirable as the form, color, and texture of their foliage will not harmonize with Box or Yew and *Crataegus pyracantha*. It will be noticed that evergreens of dark bluish green shades are suggested rather than those of yellow or brownish greens.

Two or three skillfully wall-trained Forsythia may be used on the south front underplanted with ivy; the underplanting is needed in order to make a background for the yellow flowers which without the ivy foliage are unpleasant in color immediately close to the brick wall. Two plants of Wisteria may be used at either side of the front-door steps, and these should be trained vertically in the house angles of the steps and then horizontally over the front door and its entablature to make a frame of plant material especially for this feature. On the entrance-step balustrades a controlled tangle of *Jasminum nudiflorum*, *Ampelopsis quinquefolia Engelmannii*, and Ivy should be used. The design of the balustrade was never enthusiastically accepted by the former owners. Nevertheless, they felt that a certain amount of stone should be visible so that the balustrade would not be so covered and thickened by foliage as to appear to be a hedge rather than a stone construction.

Not more than three free-standing bushes of *Forsythia intermedia spectabilis* are advised for this south-front planting, and probably one free-standing bush of *Pyracantha* will be sufficient. Two wall-trained plants of *Pyracantha* may be used on this south facade.

A high-branched tree is needed close to the southwest corner of the orangery in order to allow an unimpeded view of the building from the entrance drive and also from the building over the south lawn. If the American Elm must for some reason be replaced, the *Koelreuteria paniculata* (Golden-rain or Varnish tree) might be used, the habit of which is somewhat like *Ulmus americana*. It is a neat tree whereas the Walnut, which might be suitable in form, is not suggested on account of the coarse scale of its leafage and its nut-shedding peculiarities.

On the south wall of the building two or three plants of *Ampelopsis Engelmannii* could be used, as this is a clinging plant which is well colored in autumn. Not more than one-third of the south building-wall should be covered with Ivy and this should be kept well trimmed because if allowed to grow large and heavy it is likely to be peeled off in large flakes by heavy winds. The planting of the whole south face of the building must be kept under constant supervision for if tall growing plants such as Hemlocks (*Tsuga canadensis*) are used they will otherwise become too tree-like in their growth. The screen plants in front of the basement windows should be placed no nearer than three or four feet from their branch tips to the windows.

PLANT LIST: THE SOUTH FRONT OF THE RESIDENCE

OVER THE ENTRANCE DOORS AND ON THE STEPS

Forsythia intermedia, Border forsythia

Ampelopsis tricuspidata [*Parthenocissus tricuspidata*], Boston ivy

Jasminum nudiflorum, Winter jasmine

Wisteria sinensis, Chinese wisteria

ON THE WALLS OF THE HOUSE WESTWARD FROM THE ENTRANCE

Ampelopsis quinquefolia [*Parthenocissus quinquefolia*], Woodbine

Hedera helix, English ivy

Pyracantha coccinea, Fire thorn

WEST OF THE ENTRANCE STEPS TO THE THIRTY-SECOND-STREET GATE

Tsuga caroliniana, Carolina hemlock

Magnolia grandiflora, Southern magnolia

Buxus sempervirens, Common box

Buxus sempervirens 'Suffruticosa', Edging box

Ilex aquifolium, English holly

Ilex crenata, Japanese holly

Ilex crenata 'Fortunei' [*Ilex crenata* 'Latifolia'], Japanese holly

Ilex crenata 'Macrophylla', Big-leaf Japanese holly

Forsythia intermedia, Border forsythia

ON THE WALLS OF THE HOUSE EASTWARD FROM THE ENTRANCE

Ampelopsis quinquefolia [*Parthenocissus quinquefolia*], Woodbine

Forsythia sp., Forsythia

Hedera helix, English ivy

Pyracantha coccinea, Fire thorn

BETWEEN THE ENTRANCE AND THE ORANGERY

Magnolia denudata [*Magnolia heptapeta*], Yulan magnolia

Ulmus americana, American elm

Taxus baccata 'Repandens', Spreading English yew

Taxus baccata 'Gracilis Pendula' [*Taxus baccata* 'Pendula'], English yew

Buxus sempervirens 'Suffruticosa', Edging box

Jasminum nudiflorum, Winter jasmine

Pyracantha coccinea 'Lalandei', Leland's fire thorn

Spiraea prunifolia, Bridal wreath

Spiraea thunbergii, Thunberg spirea

ON THE WALLS OF THE ORANGERY

Akebia quinata, Five-leaf Akebia

Hedera helix, English ivy

Wisteria sp., Wisteria

GROUND COVERS

Hedera helix, English ivy

Oxalis sp., Wood sorrel

Vinca minor, Periwinkle

In this way the sky light will reach the windows while the unattractive windows themselves will be screened from the entrance drive.

On the east side of the entrance steps the following plants have been used: *Buxus suffruticosa* immediately next to the steps and *Buxus sempervirens* beyond. *Jasminum nudiflorum*, applied to the wall, and two forms of the English Yew (*Taxus gracilis* and *baccata repandens*) carry the planting to the southeast library corner. Two deciduous Spiraeas have been used, but not more than this amount of deciduous planting is advised for this section as it is important that the facade remain practically unchanged throughout the year.

On the west side of the south-entrance steps the marker plant of *Buxus suffruticosa* balances the one on the east side of the steps. These two marker plants should be matched and must balance in size, shape, and texture. Next to the *suffruticosa* marker plant, one or two large *Buxus sempervirens* are needed, as they screen not only the basement windows but also the windows of the working department of the building. A Hemlock (*Tsuga caroliniana*) is also used in this section but, again, must be replaced when it grows too large and treelike. In front of the big Box plants smaller groups of evergreen Hollies have been used: *Ilex Aquifolium*, *crenata*, *crenata Fortunei* and *macrophylla*.

The South Front of the Orangery

This area remains largely as Farrand envisioned it, with the exception of a change to the boxwood variety being grown today. After many years of slow decline, several of the English boxwood were replaced in 2019 with *Buxus microphylla* 'Little Missy', which will have the character of English boxwood while conveying improved vigor and disease resistance. While Farrand used the most appropriate plants at the time, today we have the opportunity—thanks to great strides in horticultural science over the past century—to select improved varieties that are more disease resistant and often hardier than those she could select.

The creeping fig vine (*Ficus pumilla*), which originates in one corner of the Orangery and has been meticulously trained to accent the entire interior with its unique topiary, is said to have been planted in the 1860s by an English garden designer hired by Edward Linthicum.   —JK

ON EITHER SIDE OF THE DOOR LEADING TO THE FLOWER ROOM AND THE Green Garden, a squatty plant is needed, such as a really dwarf Box, or *Taxus baccata repandens*. These are better in scale than plants which grow four or five feet high. Only an inconspicuous pair of markers is needed for this door, as it should be minimized in comparison with the south entrance door of the house and the south door of the orangery. Almost the whole south front of the orangery is covered with a groundwork of English Ivy (*Hedera helix*) on which is applied a thinly trained *Akebia quinata* but the main feature in spring is a beautiful *Wisteria*, which should be so trained that it carries its flowers high in the air as a floral entablature to the building over the tops of the windows. A flower border with Box edging was formerly planted on the south side of this building, but this was discontinued, partly in order to reduce costs of upkeep but also because the building itself is so low that any foundation planting tends to reduce still further its charming scale and lines.

Orangery front, clothed in blooming wisteria, 2021. Photograph by Sandy Kavalier.

Orangery interior, 2001.
Photographed by Joe Mills.

The South Lawn

The general shape and spatial design of the South Lawn remains as designed by Farrand. The most visible changes over the years include the exact location of trees, specifically as new oaks are routinely planted before the trees they are meant to replace have been removed. This is done to allow young trees time to establish and to gain the appropriate mass necessary to hold the design. Other alterations include the replacement of American boxwood around the center of the drive with *Buxus microphylla* 'Jim Stauffer', an improved boxwood cultivar with the form of American boxwood and high levels of resistance against boxwood blight and other prevalent boxwood diseases.   —JK

THE SOUTH LAWN IN ITS OLD FULL DEPTH WAS AN ATTRACTIVE FEATURE of the view as seen from the main south steps of the house, but for some time it has been recognized that the lawn would have to be reduced in the north and south dimension as time went on. The need for renewing the big trees and the south border plantation must result in crowding young trees into the open space which will consequently be reduced. The big Oaks south of the house and between the two gateways are gradually failing, and a policy of replacement must be started which will be unpleasant for the immediate future. The roots of the old trees spread far and wide, and it would be a foolish cruelty to interfere with them by trying to plant new large trees among the old ones. It will therefore be necessary to set out a considerable number of small new trees, understanding that certain of these will be kept as permanent plants and that others, which may not develop well, may be ruthlessly cut out in order to leave the chosen ones for the final effect. In the last ten years, more than ten of the big Oaks have vanished from the south lawn and it becomes increasingly important to replant this area not only with trees but with the border plantation which should accompany them. Probably at least fifty feet of the depth of the lawn will have to be sacrificed to this tree and border planting. It is important to do this planting if the seclusion of the place is to be preserved for the future.

Immediately opposite the front door, a stone-paved parking space was formerly adequate for the parking of a few cars, and it is thought likely to be sufficient to provide for the future except for special occasions. In time past the parking space was bordered by a hedge of *Buxus suffruticosa* but this has gradually

Narcissus blooming on the South Lawn. LA-GP-41-8, Garden Archives, Dumbarton Oaks, Trustees for Harvard University.

deteriorated until it is now shabby and unpleasant rather than attractive as a border finish to the south lawn. Someday, this Box hedge should be replaced by a low stone wall at the edge of the parking space, designed to prevent the careless driver from driving over the lawn as has been done too often in the past. This wall should be made of stone of the color and character of the paving in the parking space and should be high enough and strong enough (therefore well constructed as to foundation) to be a buffer and deterrent to a careless motorist. The low wall may be covered with Ivy, and the space behind it also carpeted with Ivy. If, as suggested, the wall is set a little distance from the present parking space, the interval between the wall and parking space should also be covered with Ivy and a stout curb set at the edge of the parking space.

The great clumps of Box opposite both sides of the front door should be preserved as long as possible; when replacement is necessary, if Box of the same quality and size are not obtainable, big Yews or possibly large Hemlocks could be used and clipped into great formal mounds. These mounds are necessary as punctuations to the front door and make good markers between which the south lawn may lie open.

Witch hazel, *Hamamelis* × *intermedia* 'Jelena'. Photograph by Sandy Kavalier.

The East (Entrance) Drive

While the Entrance Gate plantings have changed in species from the original design, Farrand's intended vision of an American version of the English landscape of expanses of lawn and trees is maintained. Along the edges, the current palette of American holly (*Ilex opaca*), southern magnolia (*Magnolia grandiflora*), deodar cedar (*Cedrus deodara*), abelia, boxwood, and witch hazel (*Hamamelis × intermedia* 'Jelena') complement the R Street border plantings and the informal design that she established. Although the individual plants have changed somewhat, visitors are still received with a framed view of the house from the gate; after entering through the plantings, these visitors are greeted with views of the expansive lawns with significant trees on either side, conveying a sense of grand scale and space. The scale of the lawn, the enclosing trees and shrubs, and the driveway and curbing all remain intact, but the erosion and displacement of the driveway pea gravel is increasingly a maintenance concern.   —JK

ON THE EAST SIDE OF THE EAST ENTRANCE GATE AN OLD NORWAY SPRUCE (*Picea Abies*) is growing. This tree is not a very long-lived species and therefore may need replacement before long. It should be borne in mind that a conifer of particularly dark foliage should be chosen, rather than one of bluish or yellowish green, as a White Pine or Colorado Spruce or *Thuja* would not be appropriate in color. The present Norway Spruce might well be replaced by another of the same sort, as this tree, often ungainly in certain positions, seems well fitted into this particular group.

To the north of this Spruce tree, a further screen to the east lawn will always be desirable, and should, if possible, consist at least partly of American or English Holly (*Ilex opaca* or *Aquifolium*). It is possible also that a small Box tree may be needed at the end of this peninsula in order to slope the plantation down, rather than making too abrupt a change from the high Hollies to the flatness of the lawn.

On the west side of the drive immediately alongside the entrance, there was formerly a splendid group of Tree-Box approximately thirty to thirty-five feet in diameter and eighteen to twenty feet high. This is the ideal plant to use in this position, as the color of its foliage and the fineness of its leafage are in harmony with the general surroundings. As this old Box clump died from old age and disease, it was replaced as a temporary measure by a group of *Magnolia grandiflora*. The

Looking south from the Orangery toward the East Drive, 1979. LA-GP-41-7, Garden Archives, Dumbarton Oaks, Trustees for Harvard University.

Magnolia was used in order to get a quick effect, and it has never been satisfactory either in scale of leaf or in character of growth as the leaves are far too coarse and shiny. Therefore, when the *Magnolia* clump can at some future time be replaced, either Box, Hollies, or Yews—or even clipped Hemlocks—would be better here than any coarse and large-leaved plant. It is essential that both the east and west sides of the entrance drive be bordered with fairly high planting near the gate, in order to mark the transition between the crowd, rush, and dust of the public street and the quiet spaciousness of the house, lawn, and surroundings at Dumbarton.

After the two gate plantations are left behind, the two lawns ought to open up to welcome the incoming guest. On the east side of the road, the east lawn needs no border planting as the essence of its charm lies in openness and easy grades. It reaches the roadside smoothly and continues down in a graceful slope almost to the east boundary of the property. The east lawn is an important part of the design of the south front of Dumbarton Oaks as it is the one large open space, and it should always be kept open for the future. Otherwise there will be no contrast between the wooded or planted parts of the property and the broad sweep of green turf. If both sides of the road are cluttered with planting, the two lawns will be too much curtailed in size and the whole composition becomes crowded and uneasy. The protection on the west side of the drive might be slightly smaller than the plantation on the east, since the south lawn will eventually become smaller and more restricted as more planting will be constantly needed in order to keep the south boundary shielded from the street.

The material chosen for the entrance drive was selected after careful consideration. The foundation of the road is of reinforced concrete on top of which was rolled a coat of tan-colored river gravel. This material was chosen because of its harmonious color, as the bluish gray of crushed rock is not friendly when used with planting material. As it was known that the gravel top, lying loosely on the surface of the concrete foundation, would be scattered by wheels of too swiftly driven vehicles, it was decided to place a frame and protective border of worn Belgian blocks to catch at least some of the gravel before it could reach the lawns on either side. This border of Belgian block serves as a frame, and it is so designed that no gutters are needed since it is built above the lawn level. The Belgian blocks do not have to be laid in a concave gutter-like shape, and so can be used as flat footways bordering the stone gravel area.

The West (Exit) Drive

With the addition of the Garden Library in 1963 under the guidance of Mildred Bliss, this portion of the garden was significantly redesigned by Ruth Havey, Farrand's successor. Grade changes necessitated a retaining wall bordering the drive, and Havey's intricate Ribbon Walk and plantings have added a more delicately detailed landscape. Interesting flowering and evergreen trees have been planted south of the Garden Library to maintain privacy and to add interest from the street below. Cherries (*Prunus subhirtella*), witch hazel (*Hamamelis × intermedia* 'Jelena'), and Japanese stewartia (*Stewartia pseudocamellia*) add deciduous interest to the backdrop of oak leaf holly (*Ilex* × 'Conaf') and deodar cedar (*Cedrus deodara*). Viburnum, hydrangea, and abelia species are repeated to harmonize this area as they are mirrored in adjacent landscapes.   —JK

AFTER LEAVING THE SOUTH MAIN-ENTRANCE STEPS AND THEIR accompanying service-wing plantation, the north side of the curving road should have a fairly close planting, as it now is, and always will be, necessary to hide the service wing and the service court and to screen the south side of the new museum wing. In this screen plantation the trees should be mainly selected from the small-leaved Oaks—such as the White Oak (*Quercus alba*), the Willow Oak (*Quercus phellos*), or the Laurel Oak (*Quercus laurifolia*)—with the accent particularly given to White Oaks. Careful note should be taken to avoid the large-leaved Oaks such as the Red Oak (*Quercus rubra*) and those of conspicuously shaped hanging, such as the Pin Oak (*Quercus palustris*). A few Scarlet Oak (*Quercus coccinea*), however, may be used; a few Tulip trees (*Liriodendron tulipifera*) may be added also. Too much of a variety should not be attempted, as trees are needed for screening and not for display of variety and contrast of foliage. The less that area is seen and noticed the more successful the plantation will be.

On the street-boundary wall a few evergreen Magnolia (*Magnolia grandiflora*) may be used west of the drive, possibly combined with a few Hemlocks and some *Cedrus Deodara*.

As Dumbarton Oaks will be more often seen in winter than summer by the public, and by students who live there during the leafless months, the flowering trees and shrubs should be less accented, and more emphasis laid on evergreen material. Flowering trees and shrubs should be used only as incidental

Garden Library and Ribbon Walk, 2013. Photograph by Kathleen Sparkes.

punctuation, especially in the area immediately surrounding streets and buildings where a permanent screen is needed. For example, *Spiraea Thunbergii* (Bridal Wreath), *Deutzia scabra*, and Jewel Bush (*Rhodotypos kerrioides*)[1] are not particularly desirable. Plants which will be found useful are Japanese Holly (*Ilex crenata*) and its varieties, such as *Ilex crenata buxifolia* and *Ilex crenata bullata* or *microphylla*, as well as Box of the *sempervirens* and *suffruticosa* types. A very occasional *Forsythia* or *Philadelphus* or *Spiraea prunifolia* might be used. American Holly (*Ilex opaca*) and the English Holly (*Ilex Aquifolium*) may be added, and an occasional plant of *Abelia grandiflora* which is attractive for autumn flower and for foliage which clings and is almost evergreen.

The trees between the exit drive and Thirty-second Street should again be White Oaks (*Quercus alba*), the American Beech (*Fagus americana*),[2] and possibly a *Sophora japonica* to replace the existing one in this neighborhood. Simplicity of planting cannot be too strongly insisted upon, as introduction of a number of varieties would be unfortunate from the point of view of both harmony of design and fitness of scale.

1   *Hortus* Third: *Rhodotypos scandens*
2   *Hortus* Third: *Fagus grandifolia*

Planting Along the R Street Wall
between the Entrance and Exit Gates

In a June 1922 letter to Mildred Bliss, Farrand noted that "while in no way should the planting on R Street look as though it were intended to close out people's view of the place, it should in effect do this, but by giving them interesting and pretty plants to look at." This guiding principle has aided our decisions on tree succession, as this area relies heavily on mature and robust evergreen and deciduous trees. While the elm trees (*Ulmus americana*) were lost to Dutch elm disease (DED), a healthy mix of American holly (*Ilex opaca*), southern magnolia (*Magnolia grandiflora*), white oak (*Quercus alba*), and swamp oak (*Quercus bicolor*) is underplanted with aucuba, abelia, boxwood, and mahonia. When the canopy opens following future tree loss, DED-resistant elms will be replanted. Planning and study are also underway to consider native substitutions such as spicebush (*Lindera benzoin*), viburnum (*Viburnum dentatum, V. nudum, V. prunifolium*), buttonbush (*Cephalanthus occidentalis*), and azalea (*Rhododendron viscosum, R. periclymenoides*) to replace the invasive understory plants. —JK

THE TREES IN THIS POSITION SHOULD REPEAT THOSE USED ON THE south lawn; and to these may be added some American Elm (*Ulmus americana*), two or three Tulip trees (*Liriodendron*), and possibly a few of the European small-leaved Linden (*Tilia cordata*). The evergreens should be chosen from the following sorts: Hemlock (*Tsuga canadensis*), *Cedrus Deodara*, and possibly a few of the Norway Spruce (*Picea Abies*) used as temporary fillers. The existing border to the R Street wall is not sufficiently deep in its present dimensions to guarantee a lasting screen, as there is not room allowed for the four or five lines of planting which are essential for a permanent border screen. Trees both deciduous and evergreen will always be needed for the border screen to veil the upper parts of the houses on the south side of R Street. The lower screening can be relied on only for hiding the first and second stories of these houses and for masking passing traffic.

Among the small evergreens to be used in this area are Holly, both American and English (*Ilex opaca and Ilex Aquifolium*), the Oregon Grape (*Mahonia*), the green-leaved (not the spotted-leaved) *Aucuba japonica*, the Portugal Laurel (*Laurus lusitanica*),[3] the evergreen Cherry (*Prunus Cerasus semperflorens*), the Japanese Holly

3 *Hortus* Third: *Prunus lusitanica*

(*Ilex crenata*), the Japanese Yew (*Taxus cuspidata*) in its various forms, and an occasional group of the semi-evergreen Honeysuckle (*Lonicera fragrantissima*) and of *Elaeagnus umbellata*. Approximately five plants of *Forsythia intermedia spectabilis* may be used between the two gates, and two good-size groups of *Jasminum nudiflorum* for winter effect, one group of *Spiraea Vanhouttei*, and possibly two groups of the ordinary green-leaved Japanese Maple (*Acer palmatum*). It is not suggested that further continuance of the use of the Maidenhair tree (*Ginkgo biloba*) be encouraged, or that Ash trees be used in the future, since the Maidenhair tree is conspicuously peculiar in its habit of growth, and the Ash does not come into leaf until late in the season and loses its foliage early in the autumn.

The English Privet (*Ligustrum vulgare*) may be used, as this deciduous shrub holds its foliage until late in the season and carries its shining black berries practically throughout the winter. The evergreens of medium height should be the English and Japanese Yew (*Taxus baccata* and *cuspidata*) and the Carolina Hemlock (*Tsuga caroliniana*). A few clumps, perhaps three or four, of *Mahonia* may be used, but the use of Norway Maple (*Acer pseudoplatanus*), *Sterculia*, and all the family of *Juniperus* is not recommended.

To cover the street wall-face between the two gates, Ivy should be planted on the upper level so that it may hang over the wall and between the interstices of the upper latticed brick. Groups of *Jasminum* are also needed, and possibly an occasional plant of *Akebia*. It has been found difficult to maintain Ivy planted on the street level, as careless hands pluck at the ends of the plants, and hands less careless have been known to dig up young plants and take them away. It has also been found necessary to spread a light wire over the R Street wall-planting to protect the creepers from the hands of passing school children who carelessly pick the leaves as they hurry to and from school.

PLANT LIST: INSIDE THE R STREET WALL, BETWEEN THE ENTRANCE AND EXIT GATES

Cedrus deodara, Deodar cedar
Tsuga canadensis, Canadian hemlock
Magnolia grandiflora, Southern magnolia
Ginkgo biloba, Maidenhair tree
Fraxinus sp., Ash
Liriodendron tulipifera, Tulip poplar
Prunus cerasus, Sour cherry
Quercus alba, White oak
Ulmus americana, American elm
Ulmus fulva [*Ulmus rubra*], Slippery elm

Taxus cuspidata 'Capitata',
    Upright Japanese yew
Ilex aquifolium, English holly
Ilex crenata, Japanese holly
Ilex glabra, Inkberry
Ilex opaca, American holly
Abelia grandiflora, Glossy abelia
Elaeagnus pungens, Thorny eleagnus
Forsythia suspensa, Weeping forsythia
Jasminum grandiflorum, Spanish jasmine

South Lawn and R Street border screening, showing the pair of American elms, prior to 1980. LA-GP-41-6, Garden Archives, Dumbarton Oaks, Trustees for Harvard University.

The Inner Edges of the East Lawn

Many of the original boxwood remain, as do the original garden beds. A small native perennial planting and birdbath have been added to the southeast corner of the plantings to honor former Dumbarton Oaks director Angeliki Laiou. This lower section of the East Lawn receives all the surface water that drains from the entire lawn, leading to wet soil which can be a challenge for many plants. Study is currently underway to reimagine this space to facilitate stormwater management while also honoring the original design intent and the memorial.　　　　　　　　　　　　　　　　　　　—JK

THE VIEW LOOKING SOUTHEAST FROM THE SOUTH DOOR OF THE MAIN building of Dumbarton Oaks shows the whole east lawn in its simplicity and sweep. It is important to realize that the planting between the surrounding walks and the sward is one of the principal features of the whole composition. Therefore evergreens, the *Deodar* and other conifers such as Box, and the fine-leaved deciduous trees like *Cercidiphyllum* or Japanese Maples, are part of the scene-painting. At the east end of the lawn, two large groups of Tree Box have been placed in converging lines in order to vary the edge of this part of the grass and to lengthen the perspective as seen from the house front. If these two clumps of Box (each one is probably over thirty feet wide and nearly twenty feet high) should ever be destroyed or have to be replaced, clipped Hemlock or Yew would probably be the nearest substitute. Some groups of about this size and of approximately this type of foliage should be maintained in these positions, as they are essential to the whole composition seen from the main vantage point at the south front of the house.

These *Cedrus deodara* flanking the East Lawn's northern edge predate Farrand's design, 2010. Photograph by Marc Vedder.

Another tree that predated Farrand, the katsura (*Cercidiphyllum japonicum*), bordering the southern edge of the East Lawn, 2021. Photograph by Sandy Kavalier.

The Path around the East Lawn

THE INNER EDGE FROM THE ENTRANCE GATE
TO THE TERRIOR COLUMN

The majestic katsura tree (*Cercidiphyllum japonicum*), likely planted by Linthicum in the 1860s and extant when Farrand began her work at Dumbarton Oaks, still holds court over this edge of the lawn, though it is beginning its natural decline. The plantings here serve the primary purpose of screening the street and framing the lawn. Some invasive species such as empress tree (*Paulownia tomentosa*), porcelain vine (*Ampelopsis brevipedunculata*), and multiflora rose (*Rosa multiflora*) are no longer used, while other species such as elm (*Ulmus americana*) have been replaced with oaks due to Dutch elm disease pressure.   —JK

THIS PLANTING MAKES A SECOND SCREEN TO THE STREET AS SEEN FROM the house and borders the lawn with a series of groups chosen for small foliage and for evergreen colors.

At the start of the walk at the entrance gate, and on its north side, is a big Norway Spruce (*Picea Abies*) which was described earlier with the entrance-driveway planting. It is the first large tree here and should be replaced by another large evergreen, probably of the same sort. A group of *Hemerocallis* are planted at the foot of the tree, as the ground is bare and unattractive if left unplanted. Next to this group plantation is an American Holly which also must be retained, as it is the screen separating the entrance road and the street from the spaciousness of the east lawn. This planting is also described in the entrance-road section.

At the little porter's lodge, Ivy and Wisteria are used on the building itself, but here again they must not be allowed to become so invasive that the lodge is turned into a green mound. Nearby a *Magnolia grandiflora* and an *Ilex opaca* are purposely planted for contrast of foliage, one large shiny and conspicuous, the other small and delicate in outline.

Between the lodge and the entrance gate, further plantings of Japanese Holly (*Ilex crenata Fortunei*) and the American Holly (*Ilex opaca*) make a veil between the gatehouse and the road itself, with a ground cover of Ivy.

In following the walk eastward from the gatehouse, on the south side of the lawn the groups are composed of *Pieris japonica*, Oregon Grape (*Mahonia*

East Lawn border path with English boxwood, looking southeast, 2021. Photograph by Sandy Kavalier.

Aquifolium), a magnificent Katsura tree (*Cercidiphyllum japonicum*), and an equally fine Japanese Maple (*Acer palmatum*). These trees and shrubs make a foliage border to the lawn difficult to equal for character and delicacy. The old plants, such as the *Cercidiphyllum* and the Japanese Maples, were growing in these places when the land was acquired by Mr. and Mrs. Bliss. The new planting has been made in an effort to bring out these beautiful old plants and yet give additional evergreen screen where the *Cercidiphyllum* and the Maple are bare in winter. Therefore, American Holly, English Holly, Oregon Grape, and Japanese Holly have been used in this tree border. The big *Paulownia tomentosa* on the southeast side of the east lawn is a tree which has often been criticized adversely, but the magnificent size of its trunk, its great height, and its purple flowers in the early summer make it so conspicuous and splendid an object that the gawkiness of its lower structure should be overlooked.

Looking northwest toward the Main House and Orangery from the edge of the East Lawn, 2021. Photograph by Sandy Kavalier.

An occasional *Forsythia*, *Viburnum plicatum*, *Philadelphus* and Common Lilac, or a *Philadelphus* and the Rose-of-Sharon, may all be used in the spaces between the evergreens.

Ground cover on either side of the walk as it turns northward past the east end of the lawn may well be continued in its mass of *Helleborus*, *Ferns*, spring bulbs, *Tulips Kaujmanniana* and *Clusiana*, Grape Hyacinth, Aconite, Snowdrops, early Narcissus, *Jonquila simplex*, and Violets, with occasional masses of *Veronica rupestris*.

Where the walk turns to the north a group of *Magnolia glauca* once screened what used to be known as the Gothic Garden from the walk. The Gothic Garden was surrounded by big clumps of Box, but these are no longer beautiful, so the old Gothic Garden becomes a pleasant tangle of the early flowering Jasmines underplanted with blue *Scilla* and other spring-flowering bulbs.

On the west side of the walk, making the east border to the lawn, several trees add protection to both the R Street and Lovers' Lane plantings: an American Elm (*Ulmus americana*), a White Maple (*Acer saccharinum*), a Cedar tree (*Cedrus atlantica*), and a large-leaved Magnolia (*Magnolia macrophylla*) which is more a curiosity than a beauty.

Much variety in this planting is not thought desirable; its main duty is to screen the house from the two adjoining streets and make a frame to the east lawn. The east lawn is one of the loveliest of the features of Dumbarton Oaks in its freedom from detail. Its generous scale and graceful slopes add quiet to the design.

PLANT LIST: THE NORTH AND WEST SIDES
OF THE CURVING PATH INSIDE THE WALL,
FROM THE ENTRANCE GATE TO THE TERRIOR COLUMN

ON THE LAWN NEAR THE ENTRANCE GATE

Picea excelsa [*Picea abies*], Norway spruce

Hemerocallis sp., Daylily

TREES, SHRUBS, AND VINES ALONG THE PATH

Cedrus atlantica, Atlas cedar

Ilex aquifolium, English holly

Ilex opaca, American holly

Magnolia grandiflora, Southern magnolia

Acer palmatum, Japanese maple

Acer saccharinum, Silver maple

Cercidiphyllum japonicum, Katsura tree

Magnolia glauca [*Magnolia virginiana*],
    Sweet bay

Magnolia macrophylla, Great-leaved
    magnolia

Magnolia stellata, Star magnolia

Pauloumia tomentosa, Karri tree

Prunus cerasus, Sour cherry

Salix elegantissima [*Salix babylonica*],
    Weeping willow

Ulmus americana, American elm

Buxus sempervirens, Common box

Pieris japonica, Japanese andromeda

Forsythia intermedia, Border forsythia

Hibiscus syriacus rosea,
    Pink Rose-of-Sharon

Lonicera fragrantissima,
    Winter honeysuckle

Mahonia aquifolium, Oregon grape

Mahonia bealei, Leatherleaf mahonia

Philadelphus coronarius, Mock orange

Rosa multiflora, Baby rose

Syringa vulgaris, Common lilac

Viburnum plicatum, Japanese snowball

Ampelopsis quinquefolia [*Parthenocissus
    quinquefolia*], Woodbine

Hosta sp., Plantain lily

GROUND COVERS AND SPRING BULBS

Aconitum sp., Aconite

Actaea rubra, Snakeberry

Galanthus sp., Snowdrop

Hedera helix, English ivy

Helleborus sp., Hellebore

Lonicera sp., Honeysuckle

Muscari sp., Grape hyacinth

Narcissus sp., Daffodil

Tulipa sp., Tulip

Veronica rupestris [*Veronica prostrata*],
    Prostrate veronica

Viola sp., Violet

The intent for this stretch of planting is like the other R Street borders: to provide diverse plant interest while screening the street view and framing the entire southeast portion of the property. Mature white oak (*Quercus alba*) and holly (*Ilex opaca*) dominate the planting, and Japanese nutmeg-yew (*Torreya nucifera*) has replaced hemlock (*Tsuga canadensis*) due to hemlock woolly adelgid pressure. The stand of bamboo mentioned by Farrand remains, but today poses significant maintenance and preservation challenges. The bamboo (*Bambusa vulgaris, Pseudosasa japonica*) is extremely invasive and must be constantly prevented from taking over adjacent plantings. Possible removal and replacement of the bamboo with a less invasive screening plant will need to be timed around the eventual replacement of several significant trees within the bamboo planting, as its removal would likely fatally impact these trees.　　—JK

THE PLANTING PROBLEM ALONG THE R STREET PROTECTIVE BRICK WALL is serious. There must always be a series of evergreen trees and shrubs as tall as possible in order that the screen from the house and the east lawn should be dense throughout the year. As the gardens are much used in winter, the narrow strip bordering the walk south of the east lawn and between it and the wall must be kept fairly constantly renewed. In this space a few Hemlocks will always be appropriate (and not costly to replace), as will groups of Tree Box (*Buxus sempervirens*) and also the small-growing Box (*Buxus suffruticosa*). There will be spaces where both English and American Holly should be used fairly freely (*Ilex opaca* and *Aquifolium*) and also Japanese Holly (*Ilex crenata Fortunei* and *microphylla*). *Aucuba japonica* (the plain leaved, not the dotted leaved) would also be suitable, and where there is light enough, a Japanese or English Yew (*Taxus cuspidata* or *baccata*) and a few plants of *Pyracantha* may fit in. The high border-screen will probably always have to be deciduous, consisting of Silver Maple (*Acer saccharinum*) and the White Oak (*Quercus alba*). Probably it would be safe to guess that in the distance between the R Street entrance and the southeast corner of the wall, about forty or fifty evergreen plants should be maintained in good condition—chosen from the varieties mentioned. They should be planted singly or in small groups of two or three, rather than in large masses. The reason the use of small groups is suggested is that they will be more easily replaced and planting therefore will be less difficult and costly to manage as a continuing problem. Among the semi-evergreens, the Japanese Privet (*Ligustrum japonicum*), the early-flowering Honeysuckle (*Lonicera fragrantissima*), the Oregon Grape (*Mahonia Aquifolium*), and *Berberis Sargentii* may be used. The deciduous material (as *Magnolia stellata*) should be distinctly secondary in its use, and may be chosen from the early-flowering *Magnolia*, the autumn-flowering Rose-of-Sharon (*Hibiscus syriacus*), the June-flowering dwarf Chestnut (*Aesculus parviflora*), the early-summer flowering Chinese Rose (*Rosa multiflora*), and the spring-flowering Japanese Quince (*Chaenomeles*, in variety),

Outer edge path bordering the East Lawn, looking west toward the katsura tree, 2021.
Photograph by Sandy Kavalier.

PLANT LIST: THE SOUTH AND EAST SIDES OF THE PATH INSIDE THE WALL
FROM THE ENTRANCE GATE TO THE TERRIOR COLUMN

TREES, SHRUBS, VINES, AND FLOWERS

Tsuga canadensis, Canadian hemlock

Ilex aquifolium, English holly

Ilex opaca, American holly

Magnolia grandiflora, Southern magnolia

Acer palmatum, Japanese maple

Acer saccharinum dasycarpum
[*Acer saccharmum*], Silver maple

Gleditsia triacanthos, Honey locust

Liriodendron tulipifera, Tulip poplar

Magnolia stellata, Star magnolia

Quercus rubra, Red oak

Ulmus americana, American elm

Ulmus parvifolia, Chinese elm

Taxus baccata, English yew

Aucuba japonica, Japanese aucuba

Buxus sempervirens, Common box

Buxus sempervirens 'Suffruticosa',
Edging box

Ilex crenata 'Fortunei' [*Ilex crenata*
'Latifolia'], Japanese holly

Ilex microphylla [*Ilex crenata*
'Microphylla'], Little-leaved
Japanese holly

Ligustrum japonicum, Wax-leaf privet

Aesculus parviflora, Bottlebrush buckeye

Berberis sargentiana, Sargent barberry

Chaeonomeles sinensis
[*Cydonia sinensis*], Chinese quince

Deutzia lemoinei, Lemoine deutzia

Forsythia intermedia, Border forsythia

Hibiscus syriacus, Rose-of-Sharon

Hydrangea quercifolia, Oakleaf hydrangea

Lonicera fragrantissima,
Winter honeysuckle

Mahonia aquifolium, Oregon grape

Philadelphia coronaries, Mock orange

Pyracantha coccinea, Fire thorn

Spiraea prunifolia, Bridal Wreath

Symphoricarpos racemosus
[*Symphoricarpos albus*], Snowberry

Symphoricarpos vulgaris
[*Symphoricarpos orbiculatus*],
Indian currant

Syringa chinensis, Chinese lilac

Syringa vulgaris, Common lilac

Viburnum plicatum, Japanese snowball

Rosa multiflora, Baby rose

Bambusa sp., Bamboo

Hosta sp., Plantain lily

GROUND COVERS

Actaea rubra, Snakeberry

Ampelopsis quinquefolia
[*Parthenocissus quinquefolia*],
Woodbine

Hedera helix, English ivy

Lonicera sp., Honeysuckle

Viola sp., Wild violet

Wisteria sp., Wisteria

East Lawn looking southeast through the cedar trees, 1979. LA-GP-14-17, Garden Archives, Dumbarton Oaks, Trustees for Harvard University.

together with a few Bridal Wreath (*Spiraea prunifolia*). *Deutzia Lemoinei* may be planted with the sweet-scented Syringa (*Philadelphus coronarius*) and the autumn Snowberry (*Symphoricarpos racemosus*), the Japanese Maple with plain green foliage (*Acer palmatum*), and the Japanese Snowball (*Viburnum plicatum*). All will find place but should be planted in as foils to the evergreens.

The ground cover may be of *Parthenocissus quinquefolia* and Ivy, Honeysuckle, Snakeberry, and wild Violets, planted in quantity sufficient to cover the bare earth in winter.

At the northeast end of the east lawn, east of the walk, marking its eastern boundary, a big grove of Bamboo should be maintained, even though an occasional hard winter kills it back to the ground meaning a consequent loss of its charm and trials for one or two seasons. This group of Bamboo is also valuable as a background to the approach to Lovers' Lane Pool and to the area under the trees surrounding the swinging seat in the Terrior enclosure.

This charming space, with its naturalistic woodland feel, remains an intimate and horticulturally diverse area in the garden. The simple metal arbor covering the urn collapsed under the weight of snow-laden ivy in 2018, but a reproduction was made from Farrand's original drawings and the arbor was replanted with several varieties of clematis. It was decided not to allow the English ivy to return, as its heavy weight would once again compromise the column and arbor. —JK

THIS IS INTENDED TO BE A SHADY PLACE IN WHICH GARDEN VISITORS MAY rest or read, separated from the flowers but yet near them. The gravel area should have suitable garden furniture: a swinging seat, a bench or two, and a few chairs and a table. Near it the "Terrior" Column and its vase make the end of the vista as seen from the south gate of the Fountain Terrace. A Chinese Elm, some small Hemlocks, Snowberry, and much ground cover should be used in this neighborhood and on the slender arches covering the "Terrior" Vase. *Clematis paniculata*, *Wisteria sinensis*, the *Parthenocissus heterophylla*, and *Jasminum nudiflorum* can all be used but kept in control, as they should not so crowd the delicate arches that they appear thick and clumsy.

Near the "Terrior" Column a Weeping Willow has seemed appropriate (*Salix vitellina*), but no herbaceous planting is needed.

A magnificent Oak tree and Maple grow near the Lovers' Lane wall. A Poplar Tulip and a Honey Locust are valuable for their high quiet screen, and should be kept, renewed, and replanted whenever the present trees deteriorate.

PLANT LIST: THE TERRIOR COLUMN ENCLOSURE

Salix vitellina [*Salix alba vitellina*],
Golden willow
Clematis paniculata,
Autumn-flowering clematis
Jasminum nudiflorum, Winter jasmine

Parthenocissus heterophylla,
Large-leaved woodbine
Wisteria sinensis, Chinese wisteria
Hemerocallis sp., Daylily

Terrior Column and *Clematis armandii*, 2021. Photograph by Sandy Kavalier.

Some original boxwood remains, although not quite enough to convey the "Cocky-Locky" aesthetic that Farrand describes. Plantings in this area harmonize well with adjacent gardens, so that it feels part and parcel with the Terrior Column walk. The apple tree remains in good health, though the large original white oak (*Quercus alba*) was removed in 2018 due to concern over its structural integrity. The triangle has been softened with the addition of *Epimedium* as a ground cover, through which peonies spring forth. The persimmons (*Diospyros virginiana*) were replanted following disruption during a water infrastructure project. The venerable deodar cedar (*Cedrus deodara*) remain and are now among the oldest trees at Dumbarton Oaks. The Yulan magnolia (*Magnolia denudata*), affectionately christened "The Bride," still blooms on what is left of its much reduced, declining form. A replacement for "The Bride" was planted just east of the existing tree and will assume its role once the original dies and is removed.

—JK

AT EITHER SIDE OF THE GATE LEADING OUT OF THE FOUNTAIN TERRACE, and balancing the Hollies on the north side of the wall, two Box plants are the markers on the south side of the wall between which the walk leads straight toward the big Apple tree. If this Apple tree should ultimately have to be replaced, another one should be planted, as the trunk of this tree as seen from the garden seems to be a wise interruption to the perspective that leads on to the "Terrior" Column and its vase.

Outside and southeast of the high Rose Garden wall, one or two *Magnolia grandiflora* may be used as screens to this high barrier, and below them flowering Dogwood—both *Cornus florida* and *Kousa*—to make an agreeable group, as they can be seen from the walk below and their foliage and flowers are also well in view from the top of the steps leading from the Rose Garden to the Fountain Terrace. The choice of *Cornus* has been made here for two reasons: both because of its spring flower, and because of its autumn color and fruit. And in winter, the gray twigs with their little shielded flower buds are pleasant against the evergreens.

On either side of the walk leading toward the Apple tree, queer old Box bushes—rather grotesque and out of shape—are purposely set irregularly on either side of the walk. This little area has been known as "Cocky-Locky's Garden," as the fantastic shapes of the Box scraps look like overgrown topiary figures and give an accent of the unexpected. It is possible that a Crabapple might be concealed among the Dogwoods, but the main body of the planting southeast of the Rose Garden Terrace should be Dogwoods feathered down with the two Jasmines, the winter-flowering *nudiflorum* and the summer-flowering *florida*.

Looking west toward the persimmon triangle, 1979. LA-GP-44-12, Garden Archives, Dumbarton Oaks, Trustees for Harvard University.

The Terrior Column, looking west, 1979. LA-GP-44-11, Garden Archives, Dumbarton Oaks, Trustees for Harvard University.

PLANT LIST: PATH EDGING FROM THE SOUTH GATE
OF THE FOUNTAIN TERRACE TO THE ORANGERY

TREES, SHRUBS, AND VINES

Cedrus deodara, Deodar cedar
Cedrus libanotica [*Cedrus libani*],
    Cedar-of-Lebanon
Tsuga canadensis, Canadian hemlock
Ilex aquifolium, English holly
Magnolia grandiflora, Southern magnolia
Acer palmatum, Japanese maple
Cercidiphyllum japonicum, Katsura tree
Cornus florida, Flowering dogwood
Diospyros virginiana, Common persimmon
Fagus sylvatica 'Purpurea', European
    purple-leaved beech
Magnolia conspicua denudata
    [*Magnolia heptapeta*], Yulan magnolia
Malus sp., Apple
Morus rubra, American mulberry
Quercus alba, White oak
Sophora japonica, Japanese pagoda tree
Tilia cordata, Small-leaved European linden
Ulmus americana, American elm

Taxus baccata, English yew
Buxus sempervirens, Common box
Buxus sempervirens 'Suffruticosa',
    Edging box
Ligustrum japonicum, Wax-leaf privet
Osmanthus aquifolium [*Osmanthus
    heterophyllus*], Chinese holly
Cydonia japonica [*Chaenomeles
    japonica*], Japanese quince
Cydonia sinensis, Chinese quince
Deutzia sp., Deutzia
Elaeagnus angustifolia, Russian olive
Forsythia intermedia, Border forsythia
Forsythia suspensa, Weeping forsythia
Hibiscus syriacus, Rose-of-Sharon
Jasminum floridum, Flowering jasmine
Jasminum nudiflorum, Winter jasmine
Ligustrum regalianum [*Ligustrum
    obtusifolium regelianum*],
    Regel's privet

The ground cover between the walk and the fantastic shapes of "Cocky-Locky" and his family—consisting of Snakeberry, *Fragaria chiloensis*, *Ampelopsis*, *Vinca minor*, and wild Violets—covers the space between the Fountain Terrace gate and the Apple tree.

As the path turns westward up the hill and passes the south gate of the Rose Garden, *Cydonia sinensis*, *Pyracantha*, *Osmanthus Aquifolium*, and *Taxus* again hug the Rose Garden wall, with one *Magnolia grandiflora* backing them up. The ground carpet is much the same as near "Cocky-Locky." Ivy, Honeysuckle, and Lily-of-the-valley edge the walk.

On the south side of the walk where the former Gothic Garden is now a tangle of Jasmine, there is a plantation of *Pachysandra* under the shrubs at the walk's curve. These shrubs are two Spiraea—*Vanhoutteiand* and *Thunbergii*—and *Deutzia*. There are also Jasmines, Box, Lilac, and *Forsythia*, with a few *Philadelphus* for the early-season scent. As the walk winds up the hill, a triangle surrounds two Persimmon trees which were among the original trees on the place.

The Persimmon is unusual in its winter bark and character. These are valuable trees, and, if possible, should be reproduced, as they are thought to

Philadelphus coronarius, Mock orange

Pyracantha coccinea, Fire thorn

Rosa multiflora, Baby rose

Spiraea anthony watereri, Anthony Waterer spirea

Spiraea douglasii, Douglas spirea

Spiraea prunifolia, Bridal Wreath

Spiraea thunbergii, Thunberg spirea

Spiraea vanhouttei, Van Houtte spirea

Syringa vulgaris, Common lilac

Viburnum lentago, Sweet viburnum

Gelsemium carolinianum [*Gelsemium sempervirens*], Carolina yellow jasmine

Paeonia sp., Peony

Paeonia albiflora [*Paeonia lactiflora*], Chinese peony

Paeonia moutan [*Paeonia suffruticosa*], Tree peony

SPRING BULBS AND GROUND COVERS

Galanthus sp., Snowdrops

Iris sp., Flag

Narcissus sp., Daffodil

Scilla sp., Squill

Sternbergia sp., Sternbergia

Actaea rubra, Snakeberry

Ampelopsis sp., Ampelopsis

Convallaria majalis, Lily-of-the-valley

Fragaria chiloensis, Beach strawberry

Hedera sp., Ivy

Jasminum nudiflorum, Winter jasmine

Lonicera sp., Honeysuckle

Pachysandra sp., Pachysandra

Vinca minor, Periwinkle

Viola sp., Wild violet

be a type which is not subject to fire blight (the curse of most Persimmon and Quince trees).

In the triangle, the winter-flowering Jasmine makes the ground cover, as the southern Jasmine, which was once attempted in this position, proved not hardy. Underneath the early Jasmine, Ivy and Vinca cover the ground, as it is necessary for this place to be presentable even in winter.

On either side of the gate leading from the south side of the Rose Garden, Box markers (inside, *Taxus* outside) have been used, but it is thought that if the inside plants are somewhat tamed as to their size, the outside markers may be omitted, so that the informal character of the planting should begin immediately outside of the gate and so make a complete contrast to the sheared and formal character of the planting within the garden.

On this walk leading up past the Rose Garden, one of the original big Oaks is still standing on the original slope. These trees must be preserved as long as possible, and plans should be made for replacing them with trees of the same sort, even though they may look ludicrously small when first set out. The big Beech on the south side of the Rose Garden makes the point of a triangle, the other points of which are the big black tree on the Beech Terrace and the third great dark Beech below the Fountain Terrace. It is realized that this Beech tree will not be a kind friend to the south side of the Rose Garden, but the disadvantage of its shade was taken into account when it was planted, as it was thought the mass and form of the tree were valuable to the whole composition, outweighing the disadvantage of its shade to the Rose planting nearby.

The edge to the walk must be kept fairly thick on its south side so that the walk cannot be seen from the east lawn. This means that Deodars or Hemlocks or Cedars-of-Lebanon, or big plants of Yew or Box, must be kept as a constant screen up to approximately opposite the east end of the Beech Terrace. Two or

"The Bride," ca. 1950s. LA-GP-35-40, Garden Archives, Dumbarton Oaks, Trustees for Harvard University.

The original "Bride," still blooming in 2021.
Photograph by Sandy Kavalier.

three Deodars in this plantation are valuable accents, and when they disappear they should be replaced, as it seems as though this is a peculiarly favorable spot for them. None of them have been winter-killed or badly injured in this plantation.

Between the evergreens and the walk, groups of deciduous shrubs, such as *Rosa multiflora*, an occasional plant of *Forsythia intermedia spectabilis*, *Cydonia japonica*, *Ligustrum japonicum*, *Elaeagnus angustifolia*, *Spiraea prunifolia*, and *Philadelphus coronarius*, may be used in moderation to give color and charm to this otherwise rather uninteresting walk. Among the deciduous shrubs, groups of Chinese Tree Peony (*Paeonia Moutan*), of fine varieties and especially chosen as to delicate colors, may be used in larger groups with *Paeonia albiflora*, the herbaceous Peony, and with small clusters of bearded Iris in shades such as the old-fashioned and still-charming variety Madame Chereau.

On the north side of the walk, between the south end of the Beech Terrace and the lower level, a group of Honeysuckle, Vinca, and Ivy overplants one of the most charming of the late-winter plantations at Dumbarton. Here Snowdrops have increased and have seeded themselves, so that in February and March this south bank is often white with the flowers. *Scilla sibirica* also has increased, and among the groups of Snowdrops there are tufts of *Narcissus* (the white varieties such as *poeticus*) and some of the paper-flower Iris, such as *Iris pallida* 'Dalmatica', Princess Beatrice, and Madame Chereau. In the later season Sternbergias show a few of their yellow cups, and *Scilla campanulata* and *Scilla campanulata albo-major*, the blue and white varieties, bloom. The Scilla are among the taller-growing bulbs used on this slope.

Immediately south of the orangery a splendid old tree of *Magnolia conspicua denudata* has been christened "The Bride," as when it is in full bloom in early April its loveliness is an enchantment. This tree should be preserved as long as it can be made to thrive and bloom well, and when its days are over it should be replaced by another as nearly like it as possible, as the sight of the white tree as seen from the R Street entrance gateway and as looked down upon from the orangery is one of the real horticultural events of the Dumbarton season.

It is almost impossible to particularize the details of the planting on this whole walk, as the deciduous trees, such as *Cercidiphyllum* and *Sophora* and American Elm, are all a part of the plantation, the reason for which is the building of a barrier between the east lawn and the walk surrounding it. When the walk was first spoken of, it was called the "Wilderness Walk," as it was like many a path in old southern places where a wilderness was an essential part of the seventeenth or eighteenth-century design.

The edging to this walk on the south and east sides should be of small Box border. When it outgrows its convenient size it should be replaced by smaller material of the same sort.

DUMBARTON OAKS GEOR

Within the image: PREND MOI TEL QUE JE SUIS

...ETOWN · D·C·

Ernest Clegg's topographical watercolor of 1935 shows a bird's-eye view from the north of the estate; the watercolor documents the composition of the Dumbarton Oaks landscape and its multiple gardens and suggests that the design of the whole is a work of art in the tradition of European villas and landscapes. House Collection, HC.P.1935.01.(wc), Dumbarton Oaks, Trustees for Harvard University.

ENCLOSED GARDENS

The Green Garden and the North Front of the Orangery

The large oak still dominating this area is more likely to be *Quercus falcata*, or southern red oak, than *Quercus velutina*, black oak, as previously thought. Farrand's recommendation that the oaks be replaced with southern magnolia (*Magnolia grandiflora*) has not been followed, as it was less important to protect the privacy of the house in its current usage than to preserve the view northward from the open terrace. Instead, a young white oak (*Quecus alba*) was planted on the opposite corner from the mature oak. Andromeda (*Pieris japonica*) and hydrangea hold the eastern edge, and the terrace itself is now planted in turfgrass, making this a comfortable shady spot in which to congregate. Farrand-designed urns decorate the corners above an intricate brick lattice wall, which encloses the space, and a plaque commemorating the friendship between Mildred Bliss and Beatrix Farrand has been placed between the urns. Its Latin translation, found in *Garden Ornament at Dumbarton Oaks* by Linda Lott and James Carder, reads: "May they see dreams springing from the spreading bough; may fortunate stars always bring them good omens. Witness to the friend of Beatrix Farrand, not unmindful of those who in a later age shall have spent their lives bringing forth the truth. This tablet has been placed by Robert Woods Bliss and his wife Mildred." —JK

THE NORTH SIDE OF THE ORANGERY DOES NOT GET ENOUGH SUN TO RIPEN buds of Wisteria sufficiently to make it flower well, and therefore the main wall-cover will probably always have to be of different sorts of *Hedera helix*. The large-leaved variety such as *cordata*, or other large-leaved sorts, are not suggested, as the scale of the foliage is far too large to be becoming to the little building.

Orangery steps, looking west from Urn Terrace, ca. 1930. LA-GP-47-32, Garden Archives, Dumbarton Oaks, Trustees for Harvard University.

The Green Garden, looking north toward Rock Creek Park, 2021.
Photograph by Sandy Kavalier.

The Green Garden, seen from the Star Garden, ca. 1930. LA-GP-22-20, Garden Archives, Dumbarton Oaks, Trustees for Harvard University.

At the base of the building a border of small evergreen plants used to be maintained, but this may not be advisable, as the border was an unfriendly one in which to grow the sorts which were attractive as a frame for the building and the terrace alongside it. Plants of *Pieris japonica* and *Ilex crenata* were used as markers to the north door and in the corners. Of these, plants will probably be needed west of the orangery building to screen the north door of the flower room and passageway. *Pieris floribunda* may also be used, although this plant is more bunchy and less graceful in its growth than *japonica*. It has, however, the merit that it is hardier and easier to maintain.

The ideal plant for use as ground cover in the center of the Green Garden is *Vinca minor*, as the color and size of the foliage seem to fit the composition perfectly. The planting has been infected by a disease, however, and it therefore will probably not be possible to replant the whole area with Vinca until the ground has

PLANT LIST: THE GREEN GARDEN

ON THE WALL OF THE HOUSE, ESPALIERED

Magnolia grandiflora, Southern magnolia

ON THE GARDEN WALLS

Ampelopsis heterophylla [*Ampelopsis brevipedunculata maximowiczii*], Porcelain ampelopsis

Ampelopsis quinquefolia 'Engelmannii' [*Parthenocissus quinquefolia* 'Engelmannii'], Woodbine

Clematis grata

Clematis paniculata, Autumn-flowering clematis

Hedera helix, English ivy

Jasminum nudiflorum, Winter jasmine

Rosa multiflora, Baby rose

Wisteria sp., Wisteria

Wisteria sinensis, Chinese wisteria

IN THE GARDEN

Magnolia grandiflora, Southern magnolia

Acer saccharinum dasycarpum [*Acer saccharinum*], Silver maple

Quercus velutina, Black oak

Taxus baccata 'Repandens', Spreading English yew

Ilex aquifolium, English holly

Ilex crenata, Japanese holly

Ilex crenata 'Fortunei' [*Ilex crenata* 'Latifolia'], Box-leaved holly

Ilex crenata 'Macrophylla', Big-leaf Japanese holly

Ilex glabra, Inkberry

Ilex opaca, American holly

Pieris floribunda, Mountain andromeda

Pyracantha coccinea 'Lalandei', Leland's fire thorn

Rhododendron mucronatum, Snow azalea

Jasminum officinale, Common white jasmine

GROUND COVERS

Fragaria chiloensis, Beach strawberry

Hedera sp., Ivy

Hedera helix, English ivy

Hedera helix 'Gracilis,' Thin-leaved English ivy

Viola sp., Violet

---

entirely recovered from the infection. In the meantime, as a temporary planting, Ivy (*Hedera helix*) may be used, or, if this be found too difficult to propagate and maintain, a temporary planting of *Fragaria chiloensis* (Strawberry) might be used for a few years. The use of this plant however, is not recommended, as it is deciduous and the planting of the Green Garden should be evergreen, in order to be attractive throughout the winter when the garden is under frequent observation from the drawing-room windows and from the upper windows of the northeast part of the house.

The walls surrounding the Green Garden are planted mainly to Ivy, on which is allowed to scramble both *Clematis paniculata* and *Clematis grata* (the semi-hardy but delicately sweet-scented sort which flowers before *paniculata*). A restrained amount of *Wisteria* is allowed on the west wall. It must be borne in mind that the stone finials to the east gates must not be covered by Ivy to such an extent that they become green and stubby lumps. The design of the stone baskets with stone fruits and birds perching should be only slightly hidden by carefully trained creepers. Occasional bunches of winter-flowering Jasmine (*Jasminum nudiflorum*) give color to the Green Garden in early spring, and a very few delicately trained plants of *Ampelopsis Engelmannii* may be used among the Ivy on the wall in order to accent the autumn. The shrubs used against the walls are the fine-leaved evergreen sorts such as *Ilex Aquifolium* and *opaca*; *Ilex glabra*, *Fortunei* and *crenata*; and an occasional plant of *Rhododendron mucronatum* (formerly known as *Azalea indica alba*). On the east wall of the drawing room are espaliered *Magnolia grandiflora*, which have to be controlled with considerable skill so that they do not become too insistent and enveloping. Some heavy planting, however, is useful in masking the awkward angle between the corner of the connecting passageway to the flower room and roof balcony and the east wall of the drawing room. This is a small re-entering angle, which, if not filled with foliage, makes an unfortunate line. On the iron brackets below the east window of the drawing room, fine-leaved Ivy should be trained so that it makes a delicate frame without hiding window light.

If bulbs are used in the Green Garden they should be of quite different sorts from those used elsewhere on the place, as the Green Garden has a quality of its own which should be emphasized by planting. Jonquils of the single campernelle sorts, the small *Narcissus poeticus*, and white Crocus were formerly planted effectively. There are also places where Squills (*Scilla siberica*) can be used; and it is possible that Star-of-Bethlehem (*Ornithogalum arabicum*) could be started, perhaps between the walks and the walls, but a warning is given that this bulb often becomes rampant.

The two big Oak trees which formerly made the great beauty of the Green Garden were the Black (*Quercus velutina*) and *Quercus rubra* or *borealis*. One of these is dead, and it is thought that the other is not likely to live indefinitely long. Therefore, the replanting of the trees in the Green Garden must be considered. As the Green Garden is no longer used for the large parties of guests who used to come to the former owners, the importance of the garden as a place of entertainment is less to be emphasized than in the past; but as the buildings are occupied more continuously in winter than in summer, the appearance of the Green Garden in winter is even more vital to consider than in the past. Probably, with all their different disadvantages, it would be wise to try two or three *Magnolia grandiflora*. It is realized that these may not withstand the cold northeast winds that sweep across this area, but if they could be made to thrive, two fine trees—one in the southeast and the other in the northwest corner of the garden—would make beautiful and permanent frames throughout the year to the northeast view from the garden over the Rock Creek ravine and toward the Connecticut Avenue bridge.

The Star Garden

This small, intimate garden has been maintained as Farrand and Bliss imagined. The white azaleas (*Rhododendron mucronulatum* 'Album'), regularly refreshed, ensure the proper scale of the plantings in the space. Though not mentioned in this book, the lantern on the wall was designed by Farrand and reproduced and replaced in 2020. Interestingly, several iterative drawings for this design exist, including schemes with two lanterns. Archival photographs show the single lantern, and in a note to Mildred Bliss in May 1938, Farrand writes: "Again here it seems to me that a boost from the Havey in thumbnail sizes will help us and I agree with you that one lantern is better than two." Thus, the decision was made to reproduce the single lantern as it was realized.　　—JK

THIS LITTLE SEMI-ENCLOSURE AT THE NORTHWEST CORNER OF THE GREEN Garden was a place designed for a more-or-less intimate, outdoor group of friends. The Chaucer quotation "O thou maker of the whele that bereth the sterres and tornest the hevene with a ravisshing sweigh" surrounds the paved circle, and set in the corners of the stone frame are lead figures of certain of the constellations: Aries, Capricorn, Pegasus, and the Phoenix. On the west wall, a lead figure of Aquarius dribbles water slowly into a yellow marble basin flanked by stone and marble seats. On the east side of the enclosure is a yellow marble table, designed for this place, but it has always seemed too large and heavy. Some day it should be redesigned and made both lower and less heavy.

The planting against the north wall of the north wing of the house is made of espaliered *Magnolia grandiflora*, set out in this position to mask blank windows on the north end of the drawing room and to screen the somewhat unpleasantly empty wall. Almost all of the planting surrounding the Star is of white *Rhododendron mucronatum* (*Azalea indica alba*). These plants should be controlled so that the little Star and its seats are not sunk at the bottom of a tall Azalea. The *Rhododendron mucronatum* will need to be replaced by smaller plants of the same sort every fifteen or twenty years, as the habit of the whole Heath family is to grow with enthusiasm for a certain number of years and then, without apparent reason, to perish inch by inch in an unsightly fashion. A few plants of *Ilex crenata* may be used among these Rhododendron if they are needed for fillers. It is desirable that the Star be somewhat separated from the rest of the Green Garden and it should not be allowed to become a clumsy and overgrown part of the unit.

The Star Garden, looking southeast, with Farrand-designed lantern, preproduced in 2020. Photograph by Sandy Kavalier.

The North Vista

THE TERRACE ADJOINING THE HOUSE

Though uncluttered and simple in its aesthetic, this space presented numerous design challenges for Farrand, and she returned to it repeatedly over her tenure at Dumbarton Oaks. Farrand's greatest obstacles were maintaining the area's role as an extension of the house, dealing with the considerable grade changes along the narrow ridge, and trying to scale the area to the house. Some plant selections have been changed to facilitate success while maintaining the design intent. English yews (*Taxus baccata* 'Repandens') have been replaced with Japanese plum yews (*Cephalotaxus harringtonia* 'Prostrata'), and hemlocks (*Tsuga canadensis*) with cypress trees (*Cupressus nootkatensis* 'Pendula'). Farrand's design focuses on scale, texture, and color with regards to the plantings, and these criteria serve as our guiding principles when making plant substitutions to mediate contemporary horticultural concerns.

—JK

THE NORTH FRONT OF THE HOUSE IS AN UNRELIEVEDLY HIGH PORTION of the building, and therefore requires careful planting and masking in order to diminish its height. The basement must be carefully screened, and heavy wall-planting used. It should be repeated that in many cases plant replacements will probably be needed every fifteen or twenty years. For example, the *repandens* Yews planted outside the basement windows and the tall Yews planted under the balconies must not be allowed to overgrow their usefulness to the point that they will either darken the windows too much or grow tall and leggy in this position where they get little or no sunlight. A constant stream of replacements must therefore be grown, so that the Yews under the windows may be kept to the right size. Between the windows, taller Japanese Yews have been apparently wisely used, but again these should be provided for in replacement crops. If they are allowed to grow tall they are not suited to the building facade, and they confuse the whole north elevation.

In the northeast and northwest angles of the house, well-trained and well-restrained *Magnolia grandiflora* should be used, pinned to the walls. The plants originally set out have grown too large. They have not been carefully watched in their training; consequently the branches stand out too far from the house wall and confuse the wall surface by their dense shadow and heavy projection.

North Vista, looking south toward the Main House from the lowest section, 2021.
Photograph by Sandy Kavalier.

Plants of approximately ten to fifteen feet in height should be used for replacement and should be chosen rather slender in their growth so that their branches may be trained and kept flattened to the wall, as is the custom with wall-trained *Magnolia* in Europe. The coarse foliage in these corners is valuable as it makes a good contrast in scale with the small-leaved Yews under the balcony. The color of the *Magnolia* foliage is harmonious with the Yews and of the same bluish green, so that the composition is not unpleasing. A few (perhaps three or four) plants of *Pyracantha* may be used on the east and west sides of the east and west wings, but other planting is not to be encouraged as the elevation of the house itself is complicated in scale and fenestration. The planting should be kept as simple as possible and carefully trained. One or two plants of *Forsythia intermedia spectabilis* may be used, wall trained and underplanted with Ivy, but no free-standing *Forsythia* is needed in the north court.

The North Vista and Main House, ca. 1925. LA-GP-34-22, Garden Archives, Dumbarton Oaks, Trustees for Harvard University.

PLANT LIST: THE NORTH VISTA

AGAINST THE WALLS OF THE RESIDENCE

Forsythia intermedia 'Spectabilis',
  Showy border forsythia
Magnolia grandiflora, Southern magnolia

Pyracantha coccinea 'Lalandei',
  Leland's fire thorn

ON THE GARDEN WALLS

Ampelopsis engelmannii [*Parthenocissus
  quinquefolia* 'Engelmannii'],
  Woodbine

Ampelopsis heterophylla [*Ampelopsis
  brevipedunculata maximowiczii*],
  Porcelain ampelopsis
Clematis paniculata, Autumn-flowering
  clematis

BORDERING THE LAWN ON THE LEVEL NEAREST TO THE RESIDENCE

Torreya taxifolia, Stinking cedar
Aesculus hippo castanum,
  Common horse chestnut
Taxus baccata, English yew
Taxus baccata 'Fastigiata'
  [*Taxus baccata* 'Stricta'], Irish yew
Taxus baccata 'Gracilis Pendula'
  [*Taxus baccata* 'Pendula'], English yew

Taxus baccata 'Repandens',
  Spreading English yew
Taxus cuspidata, Japanese yew
Taxus cuspidata 'Capitata',
  Upright Japanese yew
Ilex crenata, Japanese holly
Ilex crenata 'Fortunei' [*Ilex crenata*
  'Latifolia'], Japanese holly
Jasminum nudiflorum, Winter jasmine

BETWEEN THE FLAGSTONES

Veronica rupestris [*Veronica protrasta*],
  Prostrate veronica

On the west side of the North Vista, north of the little wing adjacent to the music room, a hedge of *Taxus baccata gracilis* has always seemed attractive. This plant is not easy to find in nurseries, nor is it easy to find a place at Dumbarton where such material can be grown. Nevertheless, a nursery for evergreens of some size seems an essential part of the whole Dumbarton unit, and some part of the Dumbarton grounds should be found for this purpose. This may be in the neighborhood of the fellows' quarters, or in some other portion of the grounds, but wherever it is established it should be carefully thought out, and, if need be, some other feature of the place should be eliminated to provide for the essential replacement nursery. The reason for insistence on a nursery at this point in the planting record is because *Taxus gracilis* in the size that is appropriate to use for replacement seems impossible to find with pendulous twigs such as have been used in the old

GROUND COVER ON THE LEVEL NEAREST THE RESIDENCE

Hedera helix, English ivy

Vinca minor, Periwinkle

Viola sp., Violet

THE LOWER TERRACES AND FRENCH STEPS

Ampelopsis quinquefolia [*Parthenocissus quinquefolia*], Woodbine

Buxus sempervirens, Common box

Cedrus libanotica [*Cedrus libani*], Cedar-of-Lebanon

Hedera helix, English ivy

Jasminum nudiflorum, Winter jasmine

GROUND COVER ON THE LOWER LEVELS

Actaea rubra, Snakeberry

Ampelopsis quinquefolia [*Parthenocissus quinquefolia*], Woodbine

Hedera helix, English ivy

Lonicera sp., Honeysuckle

Viola sp., Violet

THE TUNNEL TO THE LOWER ROAD

Buxus sempervirens, Common box

Lonicera japonica, Japanese honeysuckle

Tsuga canadensis, Canadian hemlock

Vinca minor, Periwinkle

THE WOODEN STEPS TO THE LOWER ROAD

Liriodendron tulipifera, Tulip poplar

Callicarpa purpurea [*Callicarpa dichotoma*], Chinese beautyberry

Jasminum nudiflorum, Winter jasmine

hedge. This hedge of Yew (or the temporary hedge of Hemlock which may be necessary while the *gracilis* Yews are being grown) should be clipped in steps matching the steps of the wall, rather than allowed to become a sloping hedge which would not harmonize with the wall-stepping. This stepped hedge has been decided on after many failures in dealing with this unit. The whole North Vista slopes with the natural grades, and walls have been constructed with masonry courses running parallel to the grade lines in order to minimize the considerable drop in level between the top of the steps at the north door of the round bay and the gate at the north end of the North Vista walls, a difference of fifteen to twenty feet.

On the north walls of the house, in the north court, a few plants of *Ampelopsis Engelmannii* may be used, but probably not more than two. The Ivy should be restricted to cover approximately one-third of the walls, and not be allowed to cover more than half at most. One or two fountains of the early-flowering Jasmines would be appropriate to use on the east and west court walls, and possibly a *Clematis paniculata* can be grown on the east wall of the north court where it makes a division between the north court and the Star Garden. On the east garden wall of this north court, north of the east wing, a couple of plants of *Torreya taxifolia* have been happy, and they look well in the group against the west side of the wall. At the gates leading east or west out of the north court, into the Star Garden or toward the music room, two matched plants of *Taxus repandens* should be used as gate markers and kept approximately two to three feet in height and about the same in width.

On the north balustrade of the court, the early-flowering Jasmines, Clematis, and the finer-leaved Ivies should not be allowed so to encumber the balustrade that it becomes a muffled green wall. The balustrade should show in its form as well as its height. Therefore, the creepers should be cut out in places so that the design will be evident. Again, it must be repeated that while occasional veiling of finials is desirable, it would be a complete mistake to allow them to be clothed entirely with Ivy or Clematis or creepers. The vases in the North Vista should not be allowed to have more than two or three slender trailers over their surface.

The ground cover and edging to the Yew, and the ground planting between the flags which are used for the walks of communication, should be composed of *Veronica rupestris*, moss, and white Violets, and under the windows near the Yews a frill or carpet of Ivy will probably be easiest, as well as most effective, to maintain. In all likelihood these varieties spoken of will be sufficient. If other shrubs are needed, they should be chosen from the Japanese Holly (*Ilex crenata*) and its different sorts. One or two large Japanese Yews will be useful on the east side of the court to break the somewhat abrupt transition between the height of the northeast wing and the garden wall separating the court from the Star. The basement windows under the drawing room also require considerable veiling, but the north court should not be overplanted, and a certain amount of the foundation of the building should occasionally be seen.

The Lebanon cedar (*Cedrus libani*) have been replaced with deodar cedar (*Cedrus deodara*), which grow more reliably in the Mid-Atlantic region. Deodar cedars, like all cedars, thrive in cooler climates, adding to concerns over their long-term viability as climate change presents challenges when planning for long-term tree succession. The fact that the gates leading to these terraces are less than three-feet wide adds another challenge in replacing these slow-growing trees with suitably sized successors. —JK

AT THE STEPS LEADING FROM THE NORTH COURT TO THE SECOND LEVEL, groups of Jasmines should overhang the steps and distinctly veil and muffle some of their stone work. Occasional ground cover of Ivy may be mixed with Jasmines on the slope under the balustrade; and wherever ground cover is needed, Ivy may be used at the base of the hedges or the walls. On this first terrace, the principal accent is made by the two big *Cedrus libanotica*. These should be cherished and allowed to grow as large as they will and to spread over the walls and the adjoining planting. The lower branches of these trees may have to be cut, but they should be allowed to spread horizontally as far as they will, and other plants which are in their way should be removed when they are injuring the Cedars.

The Box hedge which formerly made the enclosure to the North Vista has been replaced by a brick wall, as the Box deteriorated and became no longer either effective or attractive. The brick walls should be sparingly planted with the finer leaved Ivies, white and yellow Jasmine, and, possibly, a *Clematis montana*. Violent or exciting colors are not desirable to use on these walls, as this terrace should be very subdued in its shades of green in order to allow the dignity of the Cedars to predominate. Such muffled planting as may be needed along the foot of the walls may be either of Violets or Ivy.

The terrace intermediate between the Cedar terrace and the narrower north portion of the vista, is now enclosed by stone walls which have been placed approximately on the center-planting lines of the old Box hedges. The removal of the Box hedges and the substitution of the walls has enlarged the North Vista both in width and in length, but the proportions have been rather carefully studied so that the alteration between the scale of the old Box-bordered North Vista and the new wall-enclosed area should not be too obvious. The stone walls enclosing this intermediate terrace have been selected from stone like the stone of the garden walls on the east side of the house. The laying of the stone has been copied from the best portion of these walls, and, as before mentioned, the jointing has deliberately been made to slope with the ground in order to minimize the effect of the difference in the level on each terrace. The wall-planting of this section should be of the same fine-leaved, simple sorts of plants, like *Pyracantha* (if it can be kept so controlled as not to dwarf the walls), the yellow-flowered early Jasmine, and, for autumn color, *Ampelopsis Engelmannii*. The walls should not be overplanted, nor should material of large and heavy growth be used, as these

The North Vista, looking north from the Main House, 1959. LA-GP-34-34, Garden Archives, Dumbarton Oaks, Trustees for Harvard University.

walls are intermediate in height between the Cedar-terrace level and the extreme end of the North Vista.

The planting on either side of the steps leading from this terrace to the upper one, and also to the one below, should be bordered by Ivy; and the little brick wall dividing the levels should be crowned with Ivy, so that the red line of brick is hidden as seen from the house. The north faces of these low brick walls, however, should not be completely covered with Ivy. Seen from the north end of the vista, looking toward the house, the apparent solidity of the brick wall dividing the changes of level is valuable as a part of the whole composition.

Like the whole of the North Vista, this section changed after interventions by both Farrand and Havey after the publication of the *Plant Book*. Masonry walls were added and removed, and the area was only completed with the addition of a metal balustrade and ornament designed by Havey in 1952. In 1950, Robert Patterson replaced the wooden palings with bronze chains festooned to the wall pillars, on which wisteria has been expertly trained ever since. The plant palette was also simplified, with the wisteria, a favorite in the garden, taking center stage and the tree plantings outside of the walls visually framing the garden room.   —JK

THE HIGH STONE WALL SURROUNDING THIS PORTION OF THE NORTH VISTA is an admirable place on which to grow really well-trained wall plants. It may be wise to use some of the finer-leaved Cotoneasters, as their red berries will be handsome all winter and their fine foliage will be harmonious in scale. Climbing Hydrangea is also worthy of consideration, and possibly *Viburnum plicatum tomentosum* which is handsome in its spring flower and gorgeous in autumn color. These high walls are ideal places on which to grow choice wall-trained material. The skillful training of these plants is essential to their appearance, and while a certain number of evergreen plants are desirable on these high walls, there should also be places left where the stone shows boldly and where deciduous creepers may be allowed to fluff out and project from the wall surface.

On the wooden palings in this portion of the North Vista, light creepers should be trained so that the palings do not become completely obscured by a mass of plantings, as it is important to keep this sense of freedom from enclosure on either side of the court. This is advised not only for appearance, but also for the circulation of air. This wooden paling will later be replaced by a simple iron railing of the same height and of approximately the same spacing, as all that is required of this interruption of the wall is to give a sense of lightness and airiness without elaboration in design.

On the north end of the North Vista, it may be wise to use a few wall-trained fruit trees as a temporary measure, but it is thought that, in general, plants of more garden than edible value should be used. Therefore, the wall-trained fruit trees might well be allowed to disappear after their first usefulness is over, and the wall itself, with its planting, be allowed to take its place comparatively unnoticed in the general composition.

In its original design, the North Vista terminated in a hedge of mature boxwood, into which a tunnel of boxwood was constructed to provide a pedestrian exit. This was altered with the addition of Farrand's (and later Havey's) walls and balustrade. The slope below the North Vista is now planted in a mass of winter jasmine (*Jasmine nudiflorum*), that gently spills down the hillside and harmoniously echoes the architecture of the nearby forsythia plantation. The wood steps leading down to the path below were replaced in 2019, utilizing deodar cedar timbers reclaimed from a tree removed elsewhere on the property. —JK

ON EITHER SIDE OF THE "TUNNEL" LEADING FROM THE NORTH VISTA TO the top of the steps running northward toward the garage-court level, there should be a constantly renewed border of Hemlock (*Tsuga canadensis*), as these are needed to preserve the dark shadow seen beyond the proposed iron gate. On either side of this Hemlock planting, a ground cover should be used of Japanese Honeysuckle and *Vinca minor*; and perhaps, at its feet, there should be occasional bushes of *Callicarpa purpurea*, which would be used for their purple autumn berries. Groups of early-flowering Jasmine (*Jasminum nudiflorum*) may border the right- and left-hand sides of the wooden steps.

The North Vista, and one of the many Farrand-designed ornaments exhibited throughout the gardens, 2021. Photograph by Sandy Kavalier.

This planting of mixed evergreen and deciduous trees has performed well, providing a foil for the formality of the North Vista, and screening the Pre-Columbian Gallery and Refectory. The screening plants are constantly renewed, most recently with the addition of several *Camellia* × 'Survivor' and two white pine (*Pinus strobus*), when a mature pine fell across the North Vista in 2019, narrowly missing the North Vista walls. —JK

ON THE WEST SIDE OF THE NORTH VISTA, OUTSIDE OF THE IMMEDIATE walls, it is important to keep a perennially renewed screen of evergreens, as this side of the North Vista, if allowed to become open or screened only with deciduous material, would reveal the director's house and garage more than is desirable either for the composition as seen from Dumbarton Oaks or for the privacy of the director's house itself. Therefore, White Pines (*Pinus strobus*) and Hemlocks (*Tsuga*) should be fairly constantly planted in this west border, as both are native trees and both are likely to live at least forty to fifty years if well looked after. A dense row of planting is not necessary, but evergreen breaks in a deciduous screen are distinctly advised, as otherwise the winter prospect would be unnecessarily leafless. In former years, Norway Spruces (*Picea Abies*) had been planted on the west side of what is now the North Vista, but it is not recommended that these be replanted, as their growth is not as graceful, nor the color of their foliage as pleasant, as the Hemlock, which is the preferred tree, or the White Pine, which makes a good foil to the dark blue-green small foliage of the Hemlock. This planting of evergreens serves a double purpose, because it both makes the west side of the North Vista and the east side of the copse north of the Music Room, and separates one unit from the other, giving each privacy and background.

The Swimming Pool and Its Surroundings

The character of this space has changed perhaps more dramatically than any other garden space at Dumbarton Oaks. The removal of the weeping willows and the unsuccessful past attempts to replace them have meant that the garden is no longer a haven of shade but sits in full sun. The loss of these trees as well as adjacent shade trees on the terrace overlooking the Pebble Garden means this part of the garden is hot and dry for much of the year. The lack of shade has influenced other plantings, and the white azaleas, which should continue spilling down the hill from the Star Garden to Crabapple Hill, have been replaced with "Katharina Zeimet" roses that thrive in the full sun. Potted plants are no longer used on the swimming pool deck, but their tropical exuberance is conveyed by hardy banana (*Musa basjoo*). The hillside planting referenced by Farrand still contains historic English boxwood, among the most magnificent specimens in the gardens. Recent soil improvement work has facilitated replanting of the weeping willow (*Salix babylonica*) in 2021, and with time and shade, the reestablishment of the pool garden's character. —JK

THE DESIGN FOR THE WALL AT THE WEST END OF THE SWIMMING POOL is, again, one which has been adopted because of awkward differences in levels, combined with the need for open space surrounding the swimming pool. A straight wall with rectangular breaks in its top level would have emphasized, rather than disguised, these interesting but difficult grades. The size of the Beech under which the fountain has been placed, the curves over it, and the choice of the scale and size of the "rocaille," was all arrived at after a laborious series of experiments as to scale and fitness to both the uses of the pool and the changes of elevation. It will be noticed that the rocaille panels have been cast from the same mold. By placing the units at different heights, a non-repeating design has been achieved, as it was thought that a repeating design would look like a repeat in a small wallpaper. The color of the red marble of the fountain was chosen in order to harmonize with the cream color of the rocaille walls and the limestone copings surrounding the west end of the pool. The paving of the pool was made of limestone in order to correspond with the limestone brim of the pool itself, and this limestone paving is continued eastward from the loggia in small designs of cut limestone, as it was thought that this paving could well be as Italianate in its character as the

The swimming pool and grotto, looking west, 1944–59. Note the weeping willow on the north side of the pool. LA-GP-42-16, Garden Archives, Dumbarton Oaks, Trustees for Harvard University.

The swimming pool and loggia,
looking southeast, 1957. LA-GP-42-23,
Garden Archives, Dumbarton Oaks,
Trustees for Harvard University.

The swimming pool, looking east at sunrise, 2009. Photograph by Alexandre Tokovinine.

loggia itself. It is hoped that someday the recess in the north front of the loggia can be finished in some sort of stucco and stone ornament, as a charming series of oil-painted panels simulating frescoes, originally placed in this position, deteriorated rapidly and cruelly as the result of exposure and the dampness behind the retaining wall. The design for the ornamentation of the arches of the loggia will be interesting to work out, as designs in colored pebbles in stucco are not infrequent in Italian gardens and, combined with lead, would make an interesting unit and one unlikely to be adversely affected by its position.

The slope which lies north of the Beech Terrace and between it and the terrace overlooking the tennis court and swimming pool, is purposely planted thickly in order to give privacy to both units. The slope is rather a steep one, so that curving steps have had to be designed in order to lengthen the distance between the level of the tennis court terrace and the Beech Terrace. Principles have been followed as faithfully as possible in designing these steps so that the rise between the lower and the upper terraces would not be taken in one wearisome continuous climb. The surface of the steps and of the walk on the Beech Terrace was made in brick, in order to give some contrast to the flagged walks of the Green Garden and the Rose Garden below, and the stone paving of the tennis court terrace. It was also thought that the brick would age to a pleasant neutral color, and, as time passed, would become less and less noticeable, and would therefore more easily blend into the shades of the composition. On the slope, the principal planting is of Box, both the *suffruticosa* and *sempervirens* varieties. A large Hazel tree (*Corylus Avellana*) spreads widely and covers a large part of the bank east of the steps. Under this tree, spring bulbs of rather woodland sorts, such as *Narcissus poeticus* and *jonquilla simplex*, were planted in the Ivy ground cover that has been used on this entire bank.

As the levels on the east side of the loggia are rather difficult to manage without revealing too much of the angular corner of the northeast end of the loggia, heavy planting of Box or Yew is desirable between the west line of the steps and the east line of the loggia.

Also, a heavy screen of Box is needed at the north end of the walk leading north and south through the Beech Terrace, in order to make a reason for the sharp turn in the walk before it follows the hillside and breaks into the several flights of steps.

On the north face of the loggia, *Wisteria*, some *Clematis*, early-flowering Jasmine, and, if possible, the late-flowering Jasmine (*Jasminum officinale*) should be grown, as the scent in summer is pleasant.

North of the arcade of the loggia, which contains the dressing room for the swimming pool, groups of plants are attractive to use for summer display. Fuchsias and white Petunias seem to blend in well with the colors and to endure the north exposure with more fortitude than sun-demanding plants. Occasional pots of Heliotrope or Lemon Verbena would be attractive, adding scent as well as color.

On the west end of the swimming pool, plants of *Parthenocissus quinquefolia Engelmannii* are used to hang over the fountains in light but noncontinuous lines. These are used to break the line of the arch in which the fountain is set, and to soften this whole west end of the pool by the irregularity of their growth and their hanging veil. On the north side of the arch and on the upper level, a weeping Chinese Cherry (*Prunus subhirtella pendula*), root-grafted, is used, as this also veils the difficult levels supporting the North Vista and the west end of the swimming pool. If these banks are carefully studied, it will be seen that the planting is done to minimize the extreme change of level and the somewhat awkwardly warped slopes between the Horseshoe Pool and the northwest end of the swimming pool.

The planting between the west end of the swimming pool and the North Vista should consist mainly of *Rhododendron mucronatum*. These plants should be kept at a certain height, and when they overgrow themselves, they must be replaced by smaller ones, as Azaleas probably cannot be counted on for more than about twenty years of beauty without deteriorating and becoming leggy. This plantation of white *Rhododendron* is a part of the plantation which starts with the Star and should be considered in connection with it.

The swimming pool, looking north toward Crabapple Hill from the horseshoe steps, 2021.
Photograph by Sandy Kavalier.

The horshoe steps and fountain, ca. 1935–70. LA-GP-42-67, Garden Archives, Dumbarton Oaks, Trustees for Harvard University.

Surrounding the Horseshoe Pool, which again has been designed in order to overcome the serious difference between the levels of the Star and the swimming pool terrace, curving steps have been placed, with landings of minimum size but sufficient to break the long rise. Between the steps and the loggia, the planting space available is both small and difficult. Therefore, replacements will probably have to be made fairly frequently, as this west end of the loggia, as seen from the steps and the Star, must be screened and modified, just as the east end of the loggia must be veiled, and for the same reason. Small plants of *Ilex glabra* may be used in this small area.

On the west side of the steps, a Silver Maple (*Acer saccharinum*) also tends to break the steepness of the bank and to raise the apparent level. Further, it gives privacy to the Star, and, incidentally, carries an electric light which is placed to light the steps and the west end of the pool.

On the north side of the swimming pool, a straight line of Willows (*Salix alba vitellina*) is designed to give background to the swimming pool unit and, equally, to disguise the steep drop between the swimming pool line and the natural levels below. These Willows should be kept so trained and pruned that they do not become too large and therefore encumber the small pool unit. These trees should be renewed when they deteriorate, as it is vitally important to keep a straight "hedge line" on the north side of the pool, as the levels below the pool slope steeply in two directions—both east and north. Under the willows, a ground carpet of Ivy will probably be found the simplest to maintain. As the slope of the Crabapple Hill starts immediately northwest of the swimming pool, it is suggested that Crabapples make the planting northwest of the pool, and that in this position flowering Dogwood (*Cornus florida*) be used very sparingly.

The northeast corner of the stone-paved terrace south of the tennis court, is planted with a large American Elm (*Ulmus americana*). This tree is placed in this position not only for its shade-giving properties, but because it, again, tends to lift the grade which, also at this point, is exceedingly steep and which slopes in two directions. The trees at the northeast end of the Beech Terrace and this tree at the northeast end of the tennis court terrace are planted for the same reason: to lift the eye-line away from the natural grades and to give support to an otherwise weak corner.

The Stairway East of the Orangery

While the English and American boxwood have matured to obscure the slope, the effect is desirable as the grade change is masked and softened. This area has seen a big change in the amount of sun and shade in recent years, due to a removal of a Bliss-era white oak that provided significant shade. It is also important to note Farrand's focus on ease of movement through the garden, as this set of steps incorporates her strict principles regarding landings, riser and tread dimensions, and places of respite along the way. —JK

THE EAST END OF THE ORANGERY, OVERLOOKING THE TERRACED GARDENS, is planted with the same material used on the south side, but as the levels are difficult and unpleasant at the east end of the building, muffling plantations are needed to cover the ugly, rounded banks which support the platform. These east banks should be kept covered with some sort of plant material like Ivy and should be bordered by a small edging of fine-leaved Box (*Buxus sempirvirens suffruticosa*) which should be kept approximately twelve to fifteen inches high. This low border will mask the unpleasant slope separating the east platform and its steps.

When it is realized that the level between the floor of the Orangery and the Lovers' Lane Pool shows a drop of between forty-five and fifty feet, there will be a clearer understanding of the reasons controlling the design for the conspicuously narrow terraces and their accompanying flights of steps. The new levels were made to fit the surrounding natural levels, both to the north and south of these terraces as nearly as possible, so that the big trees on either side would not be destroyed in carrying out the garden design. The steepest slope, which lay midway between the orangery steps and the foot of the steps at the east of the Fountain Garden, explains the high walls on the west sides of both the Rose Garden and the Fountain terraces. The steps everywhere have been made with not higher than a six-inch rise, and with a fourteen-inch, or even wider, tread, as it was realized that weariness in step-climbing takes away much of the pleasure of a garden visit. It was also established as a general principle that, where possible, no flights of more than six steps should be built without a landing between the first and the next run of another six or eight steps. These landings

View to the west from the Rose Garden toward the Orangery, showing Munstead Wood, Marie Van Houtte, and Madame Anisette roses, 2021. Photograph by Sandy Kavalier.

have been made longer than three feet wherever possible, in order to give rest to the climber by a change and a pace between the series of rising runs. The runs have been constructed either of odd or even numbers. In other words, a flight of steps which starts out with an even-number of steps in its runs, is continued throughout with runs of even-numbered steps. This makes the rhythm of climbing less wearisome than if added paces have to be made on each landing in order to start the new set of steps keeping the same rhythm of right or left foot used on the first step of the first flight.

Rose Garden looking west toward the Orangery. Note the rose beds edged in boxwood. LA-GP-40-48, Garden Archives, Dumbarton Oaks, Trustees for Harvard University.

Orangery, looking east, 2010. Photograph by Alexandre Tokovinine.

The Beech Terrace

The original European beech (*Fagus sylvatica* 'Riversii') died in the late 1940s and was replaced with an American beech (*Fagus Grandifolia*), which has grown to fill the entire terrace. The form of this tree is spectacular, owing in part to the fact that its leader was lost or subordinated in its infancy, causing the lateral branches to dominate and give way to the spreading form that is atypical for this species. In fact, all three beech trees referenced in this section have been replaced—the other two with the original *Fagus sylvatica* 'Riversii'. When the American beech on Beech Terrace eventually declines, the decision will need to be made whether to replace it with Farrand's intended selection (European beech) or to continue selecting American beech for its native status and greater provision of ecosystem services. In recent years, naturalizing bulbs have been added to provide ephemeral interest in lieu of ground cover. *Chionodoxa*, *Scilla*, *Galanthus*, and other surprises await the early spring visitor.

—JK

THE BEAUTY OF THIS TERRACE IS CENTERED IN THE MAGNIFICENT *Fagus sylvatica Riversii*, the darkest of the English Beeches, which stands north of the east orangery steps.

The east wall of this terrace was placed with the controlling thought of keeping this Beech in its present position and disturbing the drainage and root system as little as possible. As the wall below the Beech was built some fifteen or twenty years ago and the tree remains in good condition, obviously the position chosen for the division between the levels has not harmed the tree in any way. If this tree should die, it should be replaced by another, as the dark Beech on this terrace and the one south of the Rose Garden and the third east of the Fountain Terrace make a flat triangle of color which is of value to the composition throughout the leafy months, and the structure of the tree in winter is almost as beautiful as its summer color. It was clear that in any position so dominated by one magnificent tree, all the other planting must be secondary and as inconspicuous as possible. Therefore, the edging to the walk which runs north and south across the terrace on its west border should probably always be of some sort of modest Box, as now.

Near the swing at the northeast part of the terrace, a weeping, flowering Cherry (*Prunus subhirtella pendula*) is set out to give a frame to this garden

The majestic American beech tree, *Fagus grandifolia*, 2021. Photograph by Sandy Kavalier.

PLANT LIST: THE BEECH TERRACE

ON THE INSIDE OF THE WALLS

Hedera helix, English ivy

Jasminum nudiflorum, Winter jasmine

Wisteria sp., Wisteria

THE HEDGE

Buxus sempervirens 'Suffruticosa', Edging box

IN THE BEDS

Fagus sylvatica 'Purpurea Riversii', Rivers' purple-leaved beech

Prunus subhirtella 'Pendula', Weeping spring cherry

Buxus sempervirens 'Suffruticosa', Edging box

Forsythia suspensa, Weeping forsythia

Wisteria sinensis, Chinese wisteria

SPRING BULBS AND GROUND COVERS

Galanthus sp., Snowdrop

Hedera sp., Ivy

Scilla sp., Squill

Vinca minor, Periwinkle

SOUTH OF THE STAIRWAY

Ilex aquifolium, English holly

Acer palmatum, Japanese maple

Magnolia conspicua [*Magnolia heptapeta*], Yulan magnolia

Buxus sempervirens 'Suffruticosa', Edging box

ON THE WALLS FACING THE STAIRWAY

Hedera helix, English ivy

Jasminum nudiflorum, Winter jasmine

Wisteria sp., Wisteria

ornament, and behind it some bushes of Box frame the north end of the terrace and divide it from the slope leading down to the level of the swimming pool.

The levels northeast of the house may seem capriciously chosen, but underlying the choice of each of these levels there has been a fundamental reason which at the time of its adoption seemed wise to heed. For example, the root grade of the big Beech tree on the Beech Terrace and the spread of its roots, control the level and the size of this terrace. Foundations of the old barn and its retaining walls seemed to give the cue for the level of the swimming pool, which is on the site of the old barnyard. The level of the tennis court—considerably lower than these other levels—was chosen as it seemed the one which was likely to make least disturbance in the surrounding levels while providing a flat place large enough for a full-sized tennis court.

The ground cover of the Beech Terrace presents a difficult problem, as it is notoriously hard to make anything grow under a Beech tree. Therefore, fairly constant replacement plants have to be ready for this particular place. They have been chosen from Periwinkle (*Vinca minor*), Ivy, and, in the spring, groups of spring bulbs such as Snowdrops and Scillas. Honeysuckle can also be used.

On the wall dividing the Beech Terrace from the Box Terrace below, Ivy may be allowed to grow but not to overgrow the open-work lattice brick. Occasional plants of Jasmine, and perhaps a *Wisteria*, may be used to minimize the sharp outlines of the brick wall and its flagstone coping. The reason brick and flagstone have been used in this wall is that its very nearness to the house makes it almost imperatively a part of the house composition. Therefore, the material used has approximated the house material; but as the gardens retreat from the neighborhood of the house, the materials used in their walls become increasingly more rustic.

On the south side of the steps leading eastward through the gardens, southeast of the orangery, a level place lies, and here a few plants of Jasmine, one or two small *Buxus suffruticosa* bushes, and a beautiful Japanese Maple (*Acer palmatum*) are quite sufficient to give the necessary amount of foliage and framing. There is also a beautiful *Magnolia conspicua denudata* which gives a lovely display of flowers in early spring.

The same *Fagus grandifolia*, forty years younger, in 1979. LA-GP-5-8, Garden Archives, Dumbarton Oaks, Trustees for Harvard University.

The Box Terrace

Now called Urn Terrace, this garden room has undergone many changes, both during the transition from private to institutional garden and in recent years. Ruth Havey oversaw the first set of changes, adding the mosaic around the urn, converting the grass pathways to brick, and substantially changing the planting scheme by adding rococo-inspired beds filled with English ivy (*Hedera helix*). In 2019, this garden room served as the first place to trial boxwood blight resistant varieties, as suitable cultivars are necessary to ensure the long-term presence of boxwood at Dumbarton Oaks. Gardeners removed the English ivy, an invasive plant, from Havey's beds and replanted them with boxwood (*Buxus microphylla* 'Little Missy'), utilizing a boxwood blight (*Calonectria pseudonaviculata*) resistant variety. The center turf panels were returned to groundcover, in keeping with Farrand's vision. Overall, this space has been simplified from a maintenance perspective by returning to Farrand's design while retaining Ruth Havey's additions. —JK

THE DESIGN FOR THIS TERRACE WAS AGAIN IMPOSED BY THE NATURAL slope of the ground and the position of the trees in the near neighborhood. The upper Beech Terrace wall was, as has been said, placed so as to avoid all possible injury to the great Beech tree which is the ornament of this upper terrace. The Box Terrace is intended to be an introduction to the Rose Garden, rather than a garden of importance on its own account. This terrace had to be narrow, as it was thought important to make the Rose Garden as large as possible in the space available. Therefore, the Box Terrace was restricted in size in order to give added breadth to the Rose Garden below. The south side of all the terraces was controlled completely by the line of trees growing to the south of them and on the slope, bordering the present gardens.

The wall dividing the Box Terrace from the Beech Terrace may have a narrow border beneath it, in which occasional clumps of flowers are grown for punctuation rather than for large effect. The center of the terrace should always be kept in plain sward, outlined by a simple Box design kept in rather small sizes. If the Box is allowed to grow too large it engulfs the scale of the terrace, which then tends to look more like a shelf than an overture to the Rose Garden. In the center of the terrace, a carved-stone vase is a copy of an old, French, terra cotta one, which

Urn Terrace with restored boxwood (*Buxus microphylla* 'Little Missy') and ground cover (*Mazus reptans*), 2021. Photograph by Sandy Kavalier.

PLANT LIST: THE BOX TERRACE

ON THE INSIDE OF THE WALLS OF THE NORTH AREA

Ampelopsis heterophylla [*Ampelopsis brevipedunculata maximowiczii*], Porcelain ampelopsis

Ampelopsis quinquefolia [*Parthenocissus quinquefolia*], Woodbine

Clematis virginiana, Virgin's bower

Forsythia suspensa, Weeping forsythia

Hedera helix, English ivy

Jasminum nudiflorum, Winter jasmine

Pyracantha coccinea, Fire thorn

Wisteria sinensis, Chinese wisteria

IN THE BEDS

Magnolia grandiflora, Southern magnolia

Magnolia stellata, Star magnolia

Prunus sp.

Buxus sempervirens, Common box

Buxus sempervirens 'Suffruticosa', Edging box

Cytisus sp., Broom

Elaeagnus pungens, Thorny eleagnus

Althaea rosea [*Alcea rosea*], Hollyhock

Thalictrum aquilegifolium, Meadow rue

BORDERS (EXAMPLES ONLY)

Aquilegia sp., Columbine

Phlox sp., Phlox

Platycodon sp., Balloon flower

Salvia sp., Sage

DOUBLE HEDGE AROUND THE CENTER BED

Buxus sempervirens 'Suffruticosa', Edging box

SOUTH OF THE STAIRWAY

Prunus sp.

Buxus sempervirens 'Suffruticosa', Edging box

Elaeagnus pungens, Thorny eleagnus

Althaea rosea [*Alcea rosea*], Hollyhock

Eupatorium coelestinum, Hardy ageratum

Salvia pratensis, Meadow clary

Syringa vulgaris, Common lilac

Thalictrum aquilegifolium, Meadow rue

EXTENDING OVER THE WALL

Magnolia stellata, Star magnolia

ON THE WALLS TO THE SOUTH OF THE STAIRS

Ampelopsis heterophylla [*Ampelopsis brevipedunculata maximowiczii*], Porcelain ampelopsis

Ampelopsis quinquefolia [*Parthenocissus quinquefolia*], Woodbine

Forsythia suspensa, Weeping forsythia

Hedera helix, English ivy

Lonicera japonica, Japanese honeysuckle

Wisteria sinensis, Chinese wisteria

BORDERING THE BEDS TO THE SOUTH OF THE STAIRS

Buxus sempervirens 'Suffruticosa', Edging box

could not endure the outdoor winter temperatures of Washington. The scale of this vase seems appropriate to the terrace. In order to give accent to the northeast corner of the terrace, an elm tree of considerable size is planted beside its northeast corner; it gives spread to an otherwise unpleasantly flat grade. The ascending lines of this elm tree seem to be what is needed to raise one's attention from the low and sloping ground to the branches of the tree.

The Box borders in the main two central designs should not be allowed to be more than a foot in height. The other borders should be kept even lower, and in order to keep a constant stream of Box replacements ready for this terrace, the Beech Terrace, the Rose Garden, and the walk surrounding the east lawn, it is recommended that numbers of Box be constantly grown so that there will be one thousand or more plants available each year for replacing overgrown material. It is thought likely that a twenty-year replacement will probably be needed for much of the Box planting, a good many of the Azaleas, and much of the Yew, and that smaller intervals will be needed between the replacements of the deciduous shrubs such as Forsythia, Dogwood, etc.

On the Box Terrace, flowers used in the border may be chosen from Columbines, *Delphinium*, *Thalictrum*, and an occasional clump of spring-flowering Tulips. On the supporting wall to the Beech Terrace: wall-trained *Wisteria*, *Pyracantha*, Ivy and the big-leaved Ivy (*Hedera helix cordata*), *Parthenocissus heterophylla* and *quinquefolia*, *Jasminum nudiflorum*—all can find small areas in which they should be kept controlled, as the wall should not be covered completely and changed into the appearance of a hedge. Probably the big-leaved Magnolia will be too large to use permanently in this position. A few plants of *Forsythia suspensa* are necessary for planting to overhang the bare walls on either side of the steps leading from the Box Terrace to the Rose Garden. These veils of *Forsythia suspensa*, interplanted with Ivy, add much to the charm of the entrance to the Rose Garden.

On the south side of the steps leading to the Rose Garden, the wall, again, must have *Wisteria* on it, Ivy (*Hedera helix cordata*), and *Clematis paniculata*. And, if necessary, flowers may be used in the minute border surrounding the retaining walls. Here, again, the same material may be used as on the north side of the steps, which cut through the terrace and divide it into unequal parts. Probably twenty or thirty plants in all will be sufficient to give the color needed during the short season. The main effect of this terrace is intended to be achieved by the wall-planting, the Box design in the center of the terrace with the stone vase, and the big Elm at the northeast corner.

The Rose Garden

This garden room has been well-maintained and preserves Farrand's intended design, which was heavily inspired by the work of Gertrude Jekyll in England. The wash of color of the rose blooms has been maintained, even while the entire Rose Garden was replanted in the 1990s, and the boxwood edging was replaced with a flagstone curbing to reduce maintenance in 1968. The flagstone walks and curbing were restored in 2019, largely reusing the historic stone. In the past few years, several of the rose beds have been renovated, including complete soil replacement with a customized blend, and new roses that have been selected for improved disease resistance in addition to their color and fragrance. Biological controls are used to minimize disease and pests while fostering a healthy and diverse habitat for beneficial insects and microorganisms. The overall effect of this work is a seemingly young, robust rose garden in a timeless setting.

—JK

THIS IS THE LARGEST OF THE TERRACES IN THE DUMBARTON OAKS GARDEN plan. As the gardens were always thought likely to be much seen in winter, the thought behind the planting of the Rose Garden has been given quite as much to the evergreen and enduring outlines and form as to the Roses, which, at their season, give added charm to this level. The Roses in the Rose Garden are really only secondary to the general design of the garden and its form and mass. The high wall, on the west side with its latticed-brick balustrade, shows the difference in the material thought appropriate to use on account of the added distance from the house and its more formal lines. The high wall is made of stone, with pilasters of brick, interrupted into panels. The pilasters of brick support the upper lattice-brick wall, which makes the parapet to the Box Terrace. This high wall is an admirable place on which to grow certain climbing Roses, perhaps a *Magnolia grandiflora*, *Clematis paniculata*, and a wispy veil of *Forsythia suspensa* narrowing the steps leading from the Box to the Rose Garden Terrace.

Big accent Box are used at the entrance steps, and there should be one large clipped Box in the middle of the garden, and probably four more large ones in two each of the north and south beds. These tall Box are intended for winter accent and as foils to the Roses growing alongside them. It is recognized that they are bad neighbors to the Roses, but this disadvantage must be taken into account when

Ambridge Rose, a delightful David Austin variety and a favorite in the Rose Garden, 2021.
Photograph by Sandy Kavalier.

The Rose Garden, 2006. Note the boxwood bed edging has been replaced with flagstone edging. Photograph by Joe Mills.

Beatrix Farrand's design plan for the Rose Garden, 1933. LA-GD-N-01D, Garden Archives, Dumbarton Oaks, Trustees for Harvard University.

the general effect of the year is considered as a whole. Accent Box are also needed in comparatively small size at both the north and the south gates, and at the opening of the steps on the east side of the garden leading toward the Fountain Terrace.

The edgings to the Rose beds should also be of Box—*suffruticosa* of varying heights—and no bed border should be allowed to grow too tall. If the Box borders to the beds are allowed to grow too large, the whole terrace becomes dwarfed and becomes a series of Box-enclosed and almost invisible beds. Therefore, the Box edgings must be replaced, perhaps over fifteen or twenty years.

The center plant in the garden may be allowed to grow to a considerable height, perhaps even fifteen feet, but the designer feels that the marker plants should be distinctly secondary in size, in order not to overwhelm the iron gates at

The Rose Garden looking northeast, 1927. LA-GP-40-11, Garden Archives, Dumbarton Oaks, Trustees for Harvard University.

Rose Garden looking west toward the Bliss crypt, through a delicate screen of Safrano roses, 2021. Photograph by Sandy Kavalier.

the north and south entrances to the garden or to so dominate the garden that the Roses are hardly noticed.

In choosing the colors for the Roses in general, the pink and salmon-colored sorts have been selected for the south third, together with a few of the very deep red ones, such as Etoile de Hollande and Ami Quinard. The center third of the garden was planted more particularly with salmon-colored and yellowish pink Roses, while the northern third was given over entirely to yellow or predominantly yellow and orange sorts.

The beds surrounding these center, formal beds have been used for small, bush Roses, such as the *polyantha*, some of the hybrid singles, and some of the smaller species Roses. The climbing Roses grown on the west wall have included Mermaid, Silver Moon, Dr. Van Fleet, American Pillar, Reveil Dijonnais, and Cl. Frau Karl Druschki.

PLANT LIST: THE ROSE GARDEN

PLANTS AGAINST THE RETAINING WALL

Ampelopsis heterophylla [*Ampelopsis brevipedunculata maximowiczii*], Porcelain ampelopsis

Ampelopsis quinquefolia [*Parthenocissus quinquefolia*], Woodbine

Clematis paniculata, Autumn-flowering clematis

Forsythia suspensa, Weeping forsythia

Jasminum nudiflorum, Winter jasmine

Wisteria sinensis, Chinese wisteria

ROSES IN THE BEDS IN FRONT OF THE RETAINING WALL

Rosa sp., Rose (American Pillar, Cecile Brunner, Dainty Bess, Dr. W. Van Fleet, Firefly, Frau Karl Druschki, Gruss an Aachen, Innocence, Irish Elegance, Katharina Zeimet, Marie Pavic, Mermaid, Reveil Dijonnais, Silver Moon)

ROSES IN THE GARDEN BEDS

Rosa sp., Rose (Ami Quinard, Ariel, Betty, Betty Uprichard, Duchess of Wellington, Ellipse, Etoile de Hollande, Federico Casas, Feu Pernet Ducher, Golden Dawn, Harry Kirk, Kaiserin Auguste Victoria, Killarney Double White, Killarney Queen, Lady Alice Stanley, Marie Adelaide, Marie van Houtte, Mme. Butterfly, Mme. Cochet-Cochet, Mme. Gregoire Staechelin, Mrs. E. C. Van Rossem, Mrs. Erskine Pembroke Thom, Mrs. Henry Morse, Mrs. Pierre S. du Pont, Peachblow, Red Radiance, Roselandia, Talisman, William Allen Richardson)

NEAR THE LARGE GATES, STEPS, TERRACE, AND BORDERS

Buxus sempervirens 'Suffruticosa', Edging box

IN THE CENTERS OF THE ROSE BEDS

Buxus sempervirens, Common box

IN THE NORTHWEST CORNER, AND ESPALIERED TO THE WEST WALL

Magnolia grandiflora, Southern magnolia

OVERHANGING THE WEST WALL

Clematis paniculata, Autumn-flowering clematis

The Fountain Terrace

The Fountain Terrace serves as a laboratory in which gardeners can experiment with new cultivars. As color was Farrand's guiding principle for this space, only the hot colors she specified are used. New plants are constantly trialed here to facilitate their use throughout the garden—and to have some fun. The beds are still changed out three times a year, with tulips in the spring, chrysanthemums in the fall, and a riot of annuals, perennials, tropicals, and bulbs in between. Recent favorites include *Tithonia rotundifolia*, *Crocosmia* 'Lucifer', and *Geum*. The Kieffer pears originally specified by Farrand for outside the eastern wall have been replanted and are used to help enclose the space, especially since the removal of the mature beech from the southeast corner. The fountains (as well as the fountains at Lovers' Lane Pool and the Ellipse) were converted to recirculating systems in 2018, dramatically reducing the water usage throughout the garden.

—JK

THIS TERRACE IS THE ONE REAL FLOWER GARDEN IN THE SERIES OF terraces sloping eastward from the main building. In the spring, probably the best bulbs to use will be Tulips, in such colors as may be found attractive. The cheapest groups which can be bought in large quantities are those of the mixed Darwins, preferably running toward the yellows, bronzes, and oranges, but if these colors prove difficult to find, the old-fashioned rainbow mixture of all sorts of colors can wisely be substituted. It should be insisted that the Tulips be supplied of sorts approximately of even height, and all of late-blooming varieties, as "misses" in the border where early-flowering Tulips come and go before the rest of the plantations are in bloom, make decided blanks in the composition. Under the Tulips, and making a border for them, annuals such as Forget-me-not, Pansies, Daisies, and possibly *Arabis*, may be set out. This garden is the one in which most change and replacement is necessary, in order to keep up the blooming effect throughout the season, and any alteration in the scheme permitting this blooming effect throughout the season would seem a mistaken economy. The area planted to the revolving series of flowers is a comparatively small one, and therefore not much space is

Fountain Terrace in full spring glory, looking north towards the Arbor Terrace, 2021. Photograph by Sandy Kavalier.

Fountain Terrace, 1979. LA-GP-18-17, Garden Archives, Dumbarton Oaks, Trustees for Harvard University.

required for propagation. After the Tulips have finished their blooming, summer-flowering annuals are planted in the borders; in the past, yellows, bronzes, blues, and primrose shades have been found attractive, rather than shades of pink, lavender, or crimson. The autumn display on this terrace, for the last years, has been an effective grouping of yellow Chrysanthemums in various shades, with bronze, deep brown, and maroon, but no pinks or whites have worked in well with this scheme of color. If the Herbaceous Border is kept up, the pink, lavender, and purple Tulips, the pink and white and lavender summer flowers, and more white Chrysanthemums may be used than on the Fountain Terrace.

The wall on the west side of the Fountain Terrace again reveals the sharp drop in level between the Rose Garden and the level of the terrace itself. Here again, the steps have been broken into three different flights in order to make the climbing not too laborious a process. Two-thirds of the way down the steps, a seat, under a lead canopy, is placed on the landing, and, when possible, is surrounded by pot plants which harmonize in color with those used in the garden.

Above: Fountain Terrace construction, 1923. LA-GP-18-5A, Garden Archives, Dumbarton Oaks, Trustees for Harvard University.

Below: Fountain Terrace, ca. 1925, showing an early Farrand design featuring sinous flagstone paths, boxwood, and hebaceous plants. Note the absence of fountains. LA-GP-18-52, Garden Archives, Dumbarton Oaks, Trustees for Harvard University.

Fritillaria imperialis 'Rubra Maxima', a favorite spring bulb on Fountain Terrace, 2021. Photograph by Sandy Kavalier.

Outside the east wall of the Fountain Terrace, Kieffer Pear trees are planted in an almost solid hedge that also stretches along the north wall. This hedge is, again, planted as a support to the garden, which otherwise would be obviously hanging over retreating grades and suspended unpleasantly in the air. The great beauty of the planting outside the east wall is a magnificent English Beech (*Fagus sylvatica Riversii*) of the darkest shade. Under this, a group of spring-flowering bulbs used to be planted—such as *Leucojum aestivum*, Aconite, and *Scilla nutans*[1] in its different shades—and later-flowering *Tiarella* and some Maidenhair and other ferns. If it be not possible to keep up this border with its formal planting, a carpet of Ivy would be easy to maintain. A plant or two of Clematis, Ivy, and fine-leaved *Parthenocissus Lowii* clothe the wall but do not cover it completely.

On the west wall, on either side of the big flight of steps, *Parthenocissus heterophylla* should be allowed to cover this area, and to cover the heavy wall enclosing the steps, as this wall, if unclothed, is over massive in its scale.

Two espaliered *Magnolia grandiflora* may be used, if not too large, in matching positions on the east side of the west wall; and two fine plants of *Taxus cuspidata*

1   *Hortus* Third: *Endymion non-scriptus*

PLANT LIST: THE FOUNTAIN TERRACE

Note: This garden is planted with seasonal flowers, from early-spring bulbs through late-autumn chrysanthemums. The following list includes only the trees, shrubs, and vines which provide the constant background to the floral display.

BELOW THE BALCONY ON THE WALLS

Magnolia grandiflora, Southern magnolia (espaliered)

Taxus baccata, English yew

Ampelopsis heterophylla [*Ampelopsis brevipedunculata maximowiczii*], Porcelain amelopsis

Ampelopsis lowii [*Parthenocissus tricuspidata* 'Lowii'], Boston ivy

Ampelopsis quinquefolia [*Parthenocissus quinquefolia*], Woodbine

Bignonia sp., Trumpet vine

Clematis paniculata, Autumn-flowering clematis

Hedera helix, English ivy

AT THE SOUTH GATE

Ilex opaca, American holly

Magnolia grandiflora, Southern magnolia

Cornus florida, Flowering dogwood

Taxus baccata, English yew

Ampelopsis lowii [*Parthenocissus tricuspidata* 'Lowii'], Boston ivy

OUTSIDE THE EAST WALL

Fagus sylvatica 'Purpurea Riversii', Rivers' purple-leaved beech

Prunus cerasus, Sour cherry

Pyrus lecontei 'Kieffer', Kieffer pear

Salix vitellina [*Salix alba vitellina*], Golden willow

---

should also be used at the back of the west borders, both to clothe and hide the heavy wall and to reduce the size of the border.

Outside the terrace on the southwest, a group of flowering Dogwood (*Cornus florida*) should be kept constantly replaced, as this feature tends to offset what is again a difficult alteration in level, and to give interest and flower in spring as well as fruit and color in autumn.

The south gate in the new, south, stone wall is marked by clipped plants of American Holly (*Ilex opaca*) at either side. These should not be allowed to become too large, as the garden is of such small size that a heavy pair of plants would throw it out of balance. The south walk is aimed almost immediately at an Apple tree which has been doctored and fed to keep it in good condition. When it fails, it should be replaced by a fair-size tree, as the effect of the rounded top and the blossomed branches, as seen from the south side of the Fountain Terrace, is a valuable part of the composition.

The transition from the brick walks of the Beech Terrace to the flagged walks of the Rose Garden and again to the grass walks of the Fountain Terrace has all been carefully thought out, and, as there is no "gangway" either from east to west or from north to south on this terrace, it should be possible to keep the turf in good condition. Two fountains are kept filled and playing during the summer season, and it is important that their curbs be allowed to become as mossy as possible, as, scrubbed and cleaned well, the curbs would look new and fresh and garish, whereas the fountains should appear to have been "found" there and to be a part of the old plan.

The Herb Garden and Wisteria Arbor

This terrace exemplifies how changes in materials do not necessitate changes in intent or purpose; moreover, it showcases a blending of styles, from Farrand's arts and crafts vision as an herb garden to Havey's baroque additions of curved Doria stone accents and steps. The herbs were abandoned, the greensward paved over in flagstone, and the terrace became a place to display potted plants during the transition from the Blisses to Harvard University. This tradition continues, as this terrace has become a showroom for antique pots designed by Eric Soderholtz, a pioneering concrete artist and friend of Farrand.

The Wisteria Arbor is inspired by a larger pavilion designed by Jacques Androuet Du Cerceau, a portion of which Farrand sketched while visiting Château de Montargis in France in the early 1900s. Reproduced in 1955, it still holds the space as its central element. In 2012, Andy Cao created a temporary installation, *Cloud Terrace*, that included a reflecting pool and cloud structure complete with ten thousand Swarovski crystals. Inspired by the reflecting pool, Dumbarton Oaks gardeners echoed its profile in flagstone following the de-installation of *Cloud Terrace* and subsequently lifted sections of the flagstone within the Doria border designed by Havey. Herbs are being reestablished in these beds, returning this space to its intent as an herb garden, while honoring Havey's embellishments. The flagstone patio was restored in 2019, and the top of the Doria bench was reproduced in 2021. —JK

THE HERB GARDEN LIES A FEW FEET LOWER AND NORTH OF THE FOUNTAIN Terrace, and this area has been considerably simplified since its original planting which proved both complicated and difficult to keep up. The middle of the area is now unbroken sward, but someday, when possible, some sort of garden ornament rather low in character might find an attractive place to break the green panel. The borders and the hedge on the north and east should be mainly of sweet-scented herbs—such as Balm (*Melissa*), Lavender (*Lavendula*), Hyssop (*Hyssopus*), Nicotine (*Nicotiana*), Catmint (*Nepeta*), Rue (*Ruta*), Wormwood (*Artemisia*)—and the scented Geraniums (*Pelargonium*—lemon, apple, etc.), Heliotrope, and Lemon Verbena. Occasional groups of *Lilium regale* may be introduced in the border, if possible, but this garden should be planted in a distinctly lower key from the Fountain Terrace. It is not a display garden but, rather, one in which shaded seats can be occupied under the big Wisteria arbor, which was placed in this position

Arbor Terrace looking west toward the wistera-clad arbor, 2021.
Photograph by Sandy Kavalier.

in order to minimize the rather overwhelming height of the stone wall which was needed to retain the northeast corner of the Rose Garden. This arbor was modified from a design of Du Cerceau (from his drawing of the garden of the Chateau Montargis). It is planted almost entirely with Wisteria, mainly of the lavender variety but with some few plants of white. The Wisteria Arbor is designed so as to be seen from below, so that the hanging clutches of the flowers will make a fragrant and lovely roof to the arbor.

In order further to make the high wall less noticeable in its austerity, a wall fountain with an old, French, lead fountain head, was designed; and a second niche, also ornamented with lead (which lead ornament needs revision), is placed to the south of the wall fountain, with a simple lead box under the arch in which a book or two might be left. This lead box has not proved practical, as the dampness in this position would ruin any book before many weeks.

The north third of the arbor is open to the slope leading to what is known as the "Goat Trail." This steep, stepped path leads down from the foot of the Beech

Abor Terrace looking north toward the balcony, 1978. LA-GP-4-12, Garden Archives, Dumbarton Oaks, Trustees for Harvard University.

The original design for Arbor Terrace featured herb beds surrounded by turf paths, 1935–45. LA-GP-4-5, Garden Archives, Dumbarton Oaks, Trustees for Harvard University.

Terrace along the north front of the Rose Garden and down a steep slope to the level of the Herb Garden and its arbor.

North of the Herb Garden, the hedge of Pear trees is continued for the same reason as the hedge of Pear trees used on the east side of the Fountain Terrace. A steep slope north and east of the garden has had to be retained by a "tow wall," which has prevented landslides that before the wall was built were frequent and destructive. The slope from the north of the Herb Garden to the Herbaceous Border below has been clothed with fruit trees, not only for their own beauty but for the purpose of hiding a steep slope and bolstering the northeast end of the Herb Garden.

The hedge surrounding the Herb Garden is made of Japanese Yew, but it is thought that in time this may wisely be replaced by either a hedge of some other material or, possibly, an iron grill or fence of some sort, which could be covered with Ivy. It is unlikely that Yew hedges can be maintained in good condition on

Farrand specified hot colors for her Fountain Terrace plant palette, a tradition that continues even while particular varieties may change, 2021. Photograph by Sandy Kavalier.

these two frontages, as they are open to wind and, also, the drainage is unfavorable to the growth of these trees which like level ground and fairly ample moisture.

The steps leading from the east gate of the Herb Garden down toward the Lovers' Lane Pool should be bordered thickly with Honeysuckle, as, again, the levels are so acute that the steps have to be both narrow and steep, and the slopes surrounding them must be veiled, and gracefully and happily planted.

On the south stone wall separating the Fountain Terrace from the Herb Garden, Clematis and Ivy are planted, the early-flowering Jasmines (*Jasminum nudiflorum*), and Honeysuckle, with an occasional plant of *Parthenocissus*.

PLANT LIST: THE WISTERIA ARBOR AND THE HERB GARDEN

THE ARBOR

Wisteria sinensis, Chinese wisteria

ON THE RETAINING WALL OF THE ROSE TERRACE

Ampelopsis heterophylla [*Ampelopsis brevipedunculata maximowiczii*], Porcelain ampelopsis

Ampelopsis quinquefolia [*Parthenocissus quinquefolia*], Woodbine

Clematis paniculata, Autumn-flowering clematis

Clematis 'Mrs. Brydon', Mrs. Brydon clematis

AT THE BASE OF THE ARBOR COLUMNS

Hedera sp., Ivy

Viola sp., Violet

AT THE GATE TO THE FOUNTAIN TERRACE

Lonicera japonica, Japanese honeysuckle

Lonicera japonica 'Halliana', Hall's Japanese honeysuckle

ON THE FOUNTAIN TERRACE WALL

Ampelopsis heterophylla [*Ampelopsis brevipedunculata maximowiczii*], Procelain ampelopsis

Clematis paniculata, Autumn-flowering clematis

Hedera helix, English ivy

Jasminum nudiflorum, Winter jasmine

Lonicera sp., Honeysuckle

SEPARATING THE HERB TERRACE FROM THE ORCHARD

Taxus cuspidata, Japanese yew

OUTSIDE THE YEW HEDGE TO THE NORTH

Pyrus lecontei 'Kieffer', Kieffer pear

THE BORDERS

Artemesia sp., Wormwood
Chrysanthemum sp., Chrysanthemum
Heliotropium sp., Heliotrope
Hyssopus sp., Hyssop
Lavandula sp., Lavender
Melissa sp., Balm

Nepeta sp., Catmint
Nicotiana sp., Tobacco-plant
Pelargonium crispum, Lemon-scented geranium
Pulmonaria sp., Lungwort
Ruta sp., Rue

The Box Walk

The Box Walk shows firsthand the complexities of managing a historic landscape while considering modern horticultural challenges. While Farrand notes that substitutions could be made if needed, she also writes that "nothing will ever be quite as beautiful as the rumpled masses of the Box as they follow the slope of the hill, but this walk must be kept bordered by some charming plant as this part of the garden design is an integral one and must not be done away with." Even in the face of general boxwood decline, and pathogens such as *Macrophomia*, *Volutella*, and the most dreaded boxwood blight (*Calonectria pseudonaviculata*, which was discovered in the gardens in 2018), we are committed to keeping one of Farrand's favorite plants, and one she used in many of the garden rooms. Gardeners have put into place strict sanitization and disease management protocols and have planted nearly five hundred *Buxus microphylla* 'Little Missy' to fill in gaps left as the original boxwood decline.

Other challenges here include the loss of several large shade trees, integral to the overall health of the boxwood beneath. Though replacement trees have been planted, the boxwood will continue to experience sun stress until the new trees provide adequate shade. Biological infusions such as compost tea, custom brewed at Dumbarton Oaks using garden-produced compost, have greatly assisted in boosting the soil microbial activity, cycling nutrients, and warding off pathogens. These infusions are brewed in-house regularly and applied throughout the garden, though the boxwood and new tree plantings are the primary recipients.

—JK

THE LEVELS OF THE BOX WALK FOLLOW THE OLD NATURAL LEVELS, AND IT IS interesting to compare this long, steep slope with the new grades surrounding it both on the east side, leading to the Herbaceous Border, and on the west side where the tennis court is enclosed by its high surrounding walls.

The slope of this walk from the north end of the Beech Terrace to the opening to the Box Ellipse is an exceedingly steep one, far too steep to be comfortable unless interrupted by steps. Therefore, the steps have been placed where the change in level seemed inevitable and to be greater than could be taken in a sloping or unstepped walk. Each side of the walk, an old hedge of the dwarf Box was

Looking south up the magnolia petal-covered Box Walk, 2021. Photograph by Sandy Kavalier.

PLANT LIST: THE BOX WALK

Koelreuteria japonica [*Koelreuteria paniculata*], Varnish tree
Lagerstroemia indica 'Alba', White crape myrtle
Magnolia denudata [*Magnolia heptapeta*], Yulan magnolia
Magnolia soulangiana, Saucer magnolia

Prunus cerasus, Sour cherry
Salix babylonica, Weeping Willow
Sophora japonica, Japanese pagoda tree
Ulmus americana, American elm
Buxus sempervirens 'Suffruticosa', Edging box
Wisteria sinensis, Chinese wisteria

planted, and this has been one of the loveliest features of the garden during past years. If, in time to come, the old Box becomes so broken and shabby that it no longer has sufficient beauty to warrant keeping it, it must be replaced by another lovely plant of fine foliage. Nothing will ever be quite as beautiful as the rumpled masses of the Box as they follow the slope of the hill, but this walk must be kept bordered by some charming plant as this part of the garden design is an integral one and must not be done away with. It may be necessary to replace the old Box with Box of smaller size and, for the future, to keep in mind the necessity for such replacements from time to time. On the whole, Box seems to fit the picture better than any other plant, and, therefore, when replacement must be done, it would seem wiser to use Box than to change to Yew or some other plant material such as Japanese Holly or even English Holly.

Between the Box Walk and the tennis court there is space for a little planting, as a backing to the Box Walk and separating it from the high wall surrounding the tennis court.

The Elm tree planted on the northeast corner of the tennis court terrace gives emphasis to this level and marks the path leading from the Box Walk to the tennis court. It also frames the Box Walk on the west side, just as the Elm tree at the northeast corner of the Urn (or Box) Terrace frames the Box Walk on the east side (the planting is east of the Box Walk, between it and the Culinary Garden). Between the west side of the Box Walk and the tennis court wall, are a Cherry (*Prunus cerasus*) and two Magnolias (*Magnolia Soulangiana* and *denudata*), and at the northwest of the Box Walk it is quite important to have a tall-growing tree of somewhat "romantic" type, marking the division between the Box Walk and the tennis court wall, which at this point rises high above the Box Walk level. The Weeping Willow which has long been there, and which has been replaced once or twice, is not particularly happy in this high and somewhat dry position, but its shape and type of foliage are so perfect for the accent that is needed at this point that it has been replaced, and should be, even at the risk of loss and fairly constant replacement.

On the east side of the Box Walk, separating it from the Orchard Hill and from the Herbaceous Border, a fine tree of *Sophora* grows on the slope, south of the Herbaceous Border and east of the long line of Box. There is also a fine Varnish

Looking north, down Box Walk toward the Ellipse, before 1960. Note the grass pathway prior to the transition to brick. LA-GP-15-13, Garden Archives, Dumbarton Oaks, Trustees for Harvard University.

tree (*Koelreuteria japonica*), which is valuable because of its graceful pinnate foliage and, particularly, because it flowers in the June season. As it lies below the Box Walk, from a position above one looks down upon the top of the tree and its creamish yellow flowers at a season when little else is in bloom.

Again, between the Box Walk and the Herbaceous Border there should be planting that would separate the two, and this may be of deciduous material. A white Crape Myrtle (*Lagerstroeviia indica alba*), such as grows between the Box Walk and the tennis court, would be well to repeat on the east side. And, again, below the Box Walk and overhanging the Herbaceous Border, a Wisteria-planted arbor is carried on wooden uprights propped into a stone wall, which holds up the bank on which the Box Walk descends.

The Box Ellipse

The Box Ellipse was substantially altered from Farrand's design by later designers, although it retains Farrand's idea for a contemplative garden. Farrand described this room as "one of the quietest and most peaceful parts of the garden," and that intent has been preserved. Farrand noted that the original boxwood hedge framing the space would need to be replaced, and several studies were conducted by Ruth Havey, but none were approved by Mildred Bliss. In 1958, the landscape architect Alden Hopkins redesigned the garden, and though some of his work (a promontory complete with fountains set into a stone knee wall) was later removed, his design of a double aerial hedge of American hornbeams suggests Farrand's intent. These trees are meticulously pruned to produce this formal aerial hedge, providing a shady spot for contemplation underneath.

After years of decline, plans to replace all seventy-six hornbeams were executed in 2019. The forty-one original trees planted by Hopkins were removed, new soil was mixed on site to exacting specifications, and new trees (which had been custom grown by a local nursery) were installed. It was decided that Hopkins's layer of pea gravel, which had served as a mulch and pathway under the trees, would not be reinstalled, as this gravel did not provide any benefit for the trees and encouraged foot traffic on the critical root zone, leading to soil compaction and tree decline. Rather, trials were conducted in 2019–20 to assess the value of several varieties of ground cover, including *Mazus reptans*, *Isotoma fluviatilis*, and *Galium odoratum*. *Isotoma* was selected for its refined aesthetic, good performance, and congruence with the design; it has now been planted in all tree beds. —JK

THE BOX ELLIPSE, INTO WHICH THE BOX WALK LEADS, IS ONE OF THE quietest and most peaceful parts in the garden. The original intention was to have the great wall of Box, fifteen or twenty-feet high, surround the somewhat irregular, turf-covered ellipse, in the center of which was the simple, jet fountain which gives a spot of light at the far end of the Box Walk. There is little visible design in the Box Ellipse, but it has been constructed out of a series of curves which appear to fit the level where an old hedge used to stand in the past years. A high bank was built on the north side of the ellipse, and a fill on the northeast corner, but the whole south and southwest and northwest sides are built on the original

The Ellipse, featuring the eighteenth-century Provençal fountain relocated from the Copse, 2010. Photograph by Alexandre Tokovinine.

The Ellipse, ca. 1956, showing Alden Hopkins's redesign, featuring an American hornbeam (*Carpinus caroliniana*) aerial hedge that replaced Farrand's American boxwood hedge. LA-GP-15-12, Garden Archives, Dumbarton Oaks, Trustees for Harvard University.

PLANT LIST: THE BOX ELLIPSE

FORMING THE ELLIPSE

Buxus sempervirens, Common box

OVERHANGING THE ELLIPSE

Acer saccharinum dasycarpum [*Acer saccharinum*], Silver maple

PLANTS ASSOCIATED WITH THE POOL

Nelumbo sp., Lotus
Zantedeschia aethiopica, Common calla lily

The Ellipse, 1978, showing Farrand's original design, including a simple fountain and American boxwood hedge. LA-GP-15-21, Garden Archives, Dumbarton Oaks, Trustees for Harvard University.

grade, and were made to fit in with the line of Silver Maples along the west, and to leave the large Silver Maple on the east undisturbed. If, in time to come, it appears impossible to replace the old "wall" with Box, it may be replaced with a stone wall of a somewhat cream-colored cast, designed with restraint and simplicity. Perhaps the wall should have a few columns on the east and west sides of the curve, and certainly an open colonnade on the north through which could be seen the far hillside of Clifton. The choice of the stone for this replacement wall must be very carefully made. The wall for the ellipse must be totally different from all the other garden walls, both in texture and color, as this part of the garden is more classic in its dimensions and character than the terraces or the immediate surroundings to the house.

At one time, planting was made under the big Box making the wall surrounding the ellipse, but it was found that the simpler the whole unit was kept, the more effective it was, and the more spacious and quiet in its design.

It is likely that many studies will be necessary before the replacement to the Box hedge around the ellipse can be satisfactorily solved, and it must be carefully borne in mind that whatever construction replaces the hedge must be placed on the center line of the hedge rather than on an academically correct ellipse, which would not fit into the natural lines or levels.

157

Kitchen Garden

INFORMAL GARDENS

Crabapple Hill

Although Crabapple Hill remains largely unchanged in terms of its layout and design, the varieties of crabapples found there have gradually changed as replacements were planted. Current favorites include *Malus* 'Donald Wyman', a well-adapted white form with red fruit introduced by the Arnold Arboretum—where Farrand first studied landscape gardening—and *Malus* 'Prairifire', a popular and disease-resistant red form with red fruit. —JK

THE PLANTING OF THIS HILLSIDE SHOULD BE KEPT MAINLY TO A FEW SORTS of Crabapple, which should be allowed to grow fairly large and not be allowed to be crowded by too many divergent sorts. At the edges of the hill and edging the walks, a few shrubs, such as the early-flowering Honeysuckle (*Lonicera fragrantissima*), *Philadelphia coronarius*, *Prunus glandulosa*, *Calycanthus floridus*, *Spiraea prunifolia*, *Ligustrum amurense*, *Kolkwitzia amabilis*, *Hibiscus syriacus*, *Cydonia japonica*, *Symphoricarpos racemosus*, *Viburnum Opulus* sterile, *Deutzia Lemoinei*, or *Ligustrum vulgare*, may be used. But the hillside itself should be kept to a comparatively few sorts of Crabapples. It is suggested that perhaps the best sorts to emphasize are *Malus spectabilis, floribunda*, Bechtel's and Bechtel's *baccata*, and possibly *theifera*[1] and *toringoides*. Too much of a variety is not likely to be successful, as the attractiveness of this part of the design should consist of the mass of flowering trees in the early season—each one having at least

1   *Hortus* Third: *Malus hupensis*

View north along the path at the top of Crabapple Hill, ca. 1940s. LA-GP-11-7, Garden Archives, Dumbarton Oaks, Trustees for Harvard University.

Crabapple Hill, looking north from the Green Garden, 2021. Note the Farrand-designed benches at the swimming pool in the foreground. Photograph by Sandy Kavalier.

PLANT LIST: CRABAPPLE HILL

TREES, SHRUBS, AND VINES

Tsuga canadensis, Canadian hemlock

Acer saccharinum dasycarpum [*Acer saccharinum*], Silver maple

Ailanthus glandulosa [*Ailanthus altissima*], Tree-of-heaven

Cornus florida, Flowering dogwood

Cornus kousa, Kousa dogwood

Crataegus cordata [*Crataegus phaenopyrum*], Washington thorn

Laburnum vulgare [*Laburnum anagyroides*], Golden chain tree

Magnolia conspicua [*Magnolia heptapeta*], Yulan magnolia

Malus angustifolia, American crabapple

Malus arnoldiana, Arnold crabapple

Malus atrosanguinea, Carmine crabapple

Malus baccata, Siberian crabapple

Malus coronaria, Sweet-scented crabapple

Malus floribunda, Showy crabapple

Malus ioensis 'Plena', Bechtel's crabapple

Malus sargentii, Sargent crabapple

Malus scheideckeri, Scheidecker crabapple

Malus spectabilis, Chinese flowering apple

Morus rubra, American mulberry

Prunus sp., Cherry

Prunus cerasus, Sour cherry

Prunus glandulosa, Flowering almond

Prunus niedzwetzkyana

Prunus serotina, Wild black cherry

Prunus shidare 'Higan' [*Prunus subhirtella* 'Pendula'], Weeping spring cherry

Prunus shidare 'Higan Zakura' [*Prunus subhirtella* 'Higan Zakura'], Flowering cherry

Prunus shidare 'Kanzan Zakura' [*Prunus subhirtella* 'Kanzan Zakura'], Flowering cherry

Prunus shigan, Flowering cherry

Prunus yedoensis, Yoshino cherry

Salix vitellina [*Salix alba vitellina*], Golden willow

Styrax japonicus, Japanese snowball

Ulmus americana, American elm

Buxus sempervirens, Common box

---

room enough to develop adequately, if not completely—and the hanging fruit in the autumn, of the different sorts which the different Apples bear. As there is another hillside planted to Cherries, it is thought desirable gradually to eliminate most of the Cherries from the Crabapple Hill, and to make the main slope west of the walk leading from the north side of the swimming pool to the Box Ellipse almost entirely an Apple grove, with perhaps two or three large trees on the north end of the hillside in order to "separate" this slope. Here a *Sophora*, or a Honey Locust tree, could well replace the *Ailanthus* which has been kept in this position because of its value as an accent. On the walk running parallel to the east wall of the North Vista, an occasional group of herbaceous plants may be used, although these are not thought vital in the general design. The sorts which would be least trouble to look after, and which would be effective

Buxus sempervirens 'Suffruticosa',
　　Edging box
Berberis thunbergii, Japanese barberry
Callicarpa purpurea [*Callicarpa
　　dichotoma*], Chinese beautyberry
Calycanthus floridus, Carolina allspice
Cydonia japonica [*Chaenomeles
　　japonica*], Japanese quince
Deutzia gracilis, Slender deutzia
Deutzia lemoinei, Lemoine deutzia
Euonymus alata, Winged spindle tree
Forsythia intermedia, Border forsythia
Hibiscus syriacus, Rose-of-Sharon
Kolkwitzia amabilis, Beautybush
Lagerstroemia indica 'Alba', Crape myrtle
Ligustrum amurense, Amur privet

Ligustrum vulgare, Common privet
Lonicera fragrantissima,
　　Winter honeysuckle
Lonicera maackii, Bush honeysuckle
Lonicera tatarica, Tatarian honeysuckle
Philadelphus coronarius, Mock orange
Spiraea prunifolia, Bridal Wreath
Spiraea vanhouttei, Van Houtte spirea
Symphoricarpos racemosus
　　[*Symphoricarpos albus*],
　　Snowberry
Syringa pekinensis, Pekin lilac
Syringa vulgaris, Common lilac
Viburnum opulus 'Sterile' [*Viburnum
　　opulus* 'Roseum'], Snowball bush
Wisteria sinensis, Chinese wisteria

GROUND COVERS

Hedera helix, English ivy
Lonicera sp., Honeysuckle

Vinca minor, Periwinkle

BULBS AND PERENNIALS (EXAMPLES ONLY)

Hemerocallis sp., Daylily
Hosta caerulea [*Hosta ventricosa*],
　　Blue plantain lily

Paeonia sp., Peony
Iris sp., flag

at various seasons, are the different sorts of Day Lilies (*Hemerocallis*), the different sorts of bearded *Iris*, and the different varieties of *Hosta*. One or two herbaceous Peonies may be used, if thought desirable, but it is pointed out that this is not likely to be a place particularly well adapted to their sun-loving growth. Shrubs such as *Euonymus alata, Cornus florida* and *Kousa*, and *Spiraea Vanhouttei, Laburnum vulgare*, and *Berberis Thunbergii* should all be kept out of the Crabapple Hill itself.

In the space between the tennis court and Box Walk and the hillside walk leading to the Box Ellipse, a greater variety and different types of shrubs may be used, as a contrast to those on the Crabapple Hill opposite. Here different sorts of *Lonicera*, as *Maackii* and *fragrantissima*, may be used; *Ligustrum, Deutzia, Kolkwitzia, Symphoricarpos, Hibiscus, Lonicera tatarica*, and *Cydonia* may also be

Malus × 'Prairifire' in flower. Photograph by Sandy Kavalier.

Malus × 'Prairifire' in fruit. Current crabapple varieties are selected for color in keeping with Farrand's design and for their disease resistance. Photograph by Sandy Kavalier.

View along the lower Crabapple Hill path, looking south toward the Pebble Garden,
ca. 1930. LA-GP-11-3, Garden Archives, Dumbarton Oaks, Trustees for Harvard University.

used, combined with a few evergreens which are needed as a permanent screen
to the little building containing the toilet and washroom for the use of the garden staff. This building should be screened from the tennis court, from the Box
Walk, and especially from the walk leading from the swimming pool to the
end of the Box Ellipse. Here a few Hemlocks (*Tsuga canadensis*) and Box (*Buxus
sempervirens*) may be used with the Privets (*Ligustrum*) which keep their foliage
latest in the year, such as *vulgare* and *amurense*. Wisteria may be planted on the
little building, and, if needed, further trees may be set out around it, although it
is desirable not to shade it too densely on account of dampness.

The ground carpet to these walks should consist of Honeysuckle, Vinca, and
Ivy, as it is important to keep the edges of the walk green and in a condition which
does not "ravel" or wash and therefore need repairing.

The Walk Leading from the Garage Court to the Box Ellipse

This walk serves as the main entry point into the gardens for maintenance equipment, thus seeing heavy traffic from the gardeners. The beautyberry has been replaced with a mass of winter jasmine, its gracefully arching branches spilling down the slope and complementing the architecture of the nearby forsythia. Fairview Hill, to the north of the walk, is one of the most inconspicuous and peaceful spaces, and it is not surprising that Jonathan Pollard (a former US intelligence analyst and convicted spy) reportedly chose one of the benches on this hill as his spot to meet with his Russian handler. It is also a great location for birdwatching, and keen observers are treated to sightings of Barred Owl, Pileated Woodpecker, Carolina Wren, and migratory birds that cross between upper gardens and the park below. —JK

THIS WALK IS THE CONNECTING LINK BETWEEN THE SERVICE END OF THE establishment and the gardens. Its planting is therefore kept quite simple and must not encroach too much on the walk, since the walk is used constantly by the trucks which take away waste material or bring supplies to the gardens. On the south side of the walk, a group of the Beautybush (*Callicarpa purpurea*) stands at the foot of the steps leading up to the North Vista. This Beautybush is of value in this position because it endures some slight shade, and also for its purple autumn fruit which lends an interest to an otherwise rather dull bank. One or two Norway Maples (*Acer platanoides*) are growing in this neighborhood, and, when possible, should be replaced by either the Silver Maple (*Acer saccharinum*) or the Sugar Maple (*Acer saccharum*), as the Norways are less attractive in their growth and autumn color than either of the other two sorts.

On the north side of the walk, big Silver Maples stand on the knoll; they should be left unencumbered by small shrubs at their base. The ground, however, is dry and hard, and should, if possible, be kept carpeted with Japanese Honeysuckle (*Lonicera japonica*) and Violets (*Viola cucullata*) and Ivy. As the walk descends the hill toward the Forsythia Dell, a few Forsythia climb up the hill to tie the hillside planting to the dell planting, and a group of the dwarf Sargent Crab (*Malus Sargentii*) fill a small triangle surrounded by the roads or paths leading to

One of several original birdbaths by Eric Soderholz, a a pioneering Maine-based concrete artisan and friend of Farrand's. Photograph by Sandy Kavalier.

Fairview Hill in fall color, looking north toward Rock Creek Park, 2020.
Photograph by Sandy Kavalier.

Fairview Hill, 1976. LA-GP-17-22, Garden Archives, Dumbarton Oaks, Trustees for Harvard University.

PLANT LIST: THE WALK LEADING FROM THE
GARAGE COURT TO THE BOX ELLIPSE

TREES, SHRUBS, AND VINES

Acer platanoides, Norway maple
Acer saccharinum dasycarpum
    [*Acer saccharinum*], Silver maple
Cornus florida, Flowering dogwood
Malus floribunda, Showy crabapple
Malus sargentii, Sargent crabapple
Buxus sempervirens, Common box

Callicarpa purpurea [*Callicarpa*
    dichotoma], Chinese beautyberry
Forsythia intermedia, Border forsythia
Ligustrum californicum [*Ligustrum*
    ovalifolium], California privet
Ligustrum vulgare, Common privet
Lonicera maackii, Bush honeysuckle

GROUND COVERS

Hedera helix, English ivy
Lonicera sp., Honeysuckle

Viola sp., Violet

PLANT LIST: THE SERVICE ROAD
TO THE ROCK WALL NEAR THE HAZEL WALK

TREES, SHRUBS, AND VINES

Acer platanoides, Norway maple
Acer saccharum, Sugar maple
Cornus florida, Flowering dogwood
Crataegus sp., Hawthorn
Liriodendron tulipifera, Tulip poplar
Morus rubra, American mulberry
Sophora japonica, Japanese pagoda tree
Kalmia latifolia, Mountain laurel
Rhododendron maximum, Rosebay

Benzoin aestivale [*Lindera benzoin*],
    Spicebush
Callicarpa purpurea
    [*Callicarpa dichotoma*],
    Chinese beautyberry
Calluna vulgaris, Heather
Cytisus albus, Portuguese broom
Vaccinium corymbosum,
    Highbush blueberry

GROUND COVER

Ophiopogon sp., Lilyturf

BULBS AND PERENNIALS

Iris sp., Flag
Tulipa sp., Tulip
Viola sp., Violet

ON THE PROPERTY FENCE

Lonicera japonica, Japanese honeysuckle

the ellipse and the dell. These dwarf Crabs will probably need renewal every fifteen or twenty years, and as this variety of Crab does not come true from seed, it had better be reproduced from cuttings in order to assure a continuation of the dwarf form in this position.

On the south side of the path and between the path and the little mens' toilet-room house, a few plants of evergreens such as Box, the common English Privet (*Ligustrum vulgare*), Privet (*Ligustrum californicum*), and the red-fruited *Lonicera Maackii* are used, and should be continued, as a screen in this position is essential.

The branch from this walk leads over the hill to the Hazel Walk. After passing the knoll with its fine group of Silver Maples (*Acer saccharinum*), a mixed plantation of deciduous trees, such as the Sugar Maple (*Acer saccharum*) and Tulip tree (*Liriodendron tulipifera*), will tie the upper planting to the planting near the Hazel Walk. The use of Norway Maples is deplored if Silver or Sugar Maples can be used in their stead.

On the south, top side of the rock wall which lies to the west of the road leading toward the Hazel Walk, a "shelf" has been prepared where a few of the acid-soil plants of the north have grown with some success. This area has been made acid by applications of peat, and therefore Heather (*Calluna vulgaris*), Blueberry (*Vaccinium corymbosum*), and a few yellow Brooms (*Cytisus albus*) appear to be doing well, although the climate is rather hot for this type of material.

Originally the wall was planned to be planted to rock-garden material, but the climate at Washington proves to be so hot that the care of this attractive, but not over-vigorous group proves too heavy a burden to impose on any but those who are personally interested in Alpines. Therefore, as time goes on, the wall is likely to be forgotten, except as a means of holding up the bank and making possible a level walk below it. The wall itself may be covered with Ivy, as the fence on the property line is covered with Japanese Honeysuckle and Grapes. Above the wall, however, there will always be a place where Violets, the small Tulips, and the dwarf Iris such as *cristata* and *pumila*, will grow well and look attractive—also Narcissus.

Between the wall and the greenhouses there should be a heavy planting of *Rhododendron maximum*, maintained as a screen and border to the ugly foundations of glass houses which, in themselves, are seldom attractive. One or two of the Mulberry (*Morus rubra*) may be kept in this neighborhood, as it is a favorite haunt of birds. They love the fruit. There is also a *Sophora japonica* which appears happy in this position, and its habit and grace are an addition to the plantation.

The Forsythia Dell

Walking amid the acre of forsythia in full bloom, seemingly lost in the winding paths, one is struck by the impact of repeating scale and texture, unexpected from such a cosmopolitan plant. Indeed, the weeping architecture of these plants was of primary import to Farrand, and gardeners have resumed hard annual pruning to ensure an abundance of juvenile growth each year. This planting was severely impacted by a stormwater project in 2017–18 that left large swaths of bare ground following the installation of new storm lines and catch basins. Fortunately, the forsythia has recovered, following replanting of over three hundred forsythia plants. Forsythia Dell consists primarily of *Forsythia × intermedia* 'Spectabilis' that is propagated in-house to prevent possible contamination with another variety, as forsythia varieties are often mislabeled and confused in the nursery trade. On the slope between Forsythia Dell and the Ellipse, *Forsythia × intermedia* 'Beatrix Farrand' has been planted. This Arnold Arboretum introduction produces longer stems with a more pronounced weeping characteristic and abundant blooms.   —JK

THE STEPS LEADING THROUGH THE FORSYTHIA PLANTATION FOLLOW AN old track down the hill which was so steep that more steps have been necessary than are either attractive or agreeable, but the drop from the top of the Forsythia Dell to the streamside is so violent that a sloping walk would have resembled a slide rather than a passive walk. The bottom of this part of old Dumbarton is now in the public park, but its character is shaped by the upper part of the walk which is still in the gardens of Dumbarton. The Forsythia should be kept pruned each year, so that the heavy wood is taken out of the plants and so that they are not allowed to become too massive or invasive. If all the modeling of the hill is obscured by the mass of Forsythia, it becomes only a tangled, even if lovely, group of planting. The modeling of the hillside is an essential part of its beauty.

It is essential that the Forsythia be kept all alike in variety, as the intrusion of different shades of flower and different habits of shrub-growth would be unpleasant and would spoil the glory of the golden flowers piled up on either side of the walk leading to the lower stream. It is thought likely that the Forsythia plants can be carefully pruned and kept in condition for a considerable number of years, perhaps twenty or more; but where a plant distinctly shows it has outlived its beauty, it should be replaced by some of the rooted runners from the hillside.

Forsythia Dell, looking east from Fairview Hill, 2021. Photograph by Sandy Kavalier.

Forsythia Dell, looking west from the Ellipse, 1959. LA-GP-17-11, Garden Archives, Dumbarton Oaks, Trustees for Harvard University.

The Walk Along the North Side of the Box Ellipse, Over the Catalogue Hill

The roses mentioned in this area no longer exist, as the heavy shade from adjacent trees prevents their success. Instead, the portion of the slope closest to Forsythia Dell has been planted with *Forsythia × intermedia* 'Beatrix Farrand'. Several dogwood (*Cornus florida* 'Appalachian Spring') and a specimen Japanese apricot (*Prunus mume*) provide structure, and to the east, a magnificent *Magnolia denudata* 'Purple Eye' has been allowed to become the dominant feature. —JK

THE IDEA UNDERLYING THE PLANTING OF THE NORTH SLOPE OF THIS hillside is that it should consist almost entirely of different sorts of species and old-fashioned Roses, such as *Rosa rubiginosa* and its hybrids (Anne of Geierstein, Brenda, Lady Penzance, Lord Penzance, Meg Merrilies), *Rosa rugosa* and its hybrids (Conrad Ferdinand Meyer, Blanc Double de Coubert, Mme. Georges Bruant, Agnes), *Rosa Hugonis, Moyesii, centifolia, spinosissima, spinosissima altaica,* Harison's Yellow, and Persian Yellow. The lower-growing sorts of these should be planted next to the walk, north of the hillside and west of the catalogue house. The taller growing sorts, such as the *eglanteria* and its hybrids, should be planted at the top of the hill, where they are not likely to give thorny interference to passersby.

It is suggested that this Rose hill be kept free of unrelated groups of perennials, such as Day Lilies (*Hemerocallis*), Peonies, etc., but an occasional tuft of single Hollyhock will add interest to the summer dullness of the hillside.

On the east slope of the hill is a large Silver Maple (*Acer sacchannum dasycarpum*), and under it and its nearby bench a group of Lily-of-the-valley, Violets, and Honeysuckle will make an attractive clothing to the bank under the spread of the tree branches.

On the west end of the walk, where the Rose hillside is hidden at the approach to the Forsythia Dell, the edges of the walk are planted thickly with *Forsythia intermedia spectabilis*, as this is more especially the approach to the Forsythia walk than it is the entrance to the Rose hillside.

Occasional Mulleins may be used in the Rose hillside as incidental accents, just as Hollyhocks are intended to punctuate the dull mid-season, but Cherries, Matrimony Vine (*Lycium halimifolium*), and such material as *Hosta* or *Astilbe* should not be used.

Looking west toward the Catalogue House from Cherry Hill, 2021.
Photograph by Sandy Kavalier.

PLANT LIST: THE WALK BORDERING THE BOX ELLIPSE
AND OVERLOOKING THE CATALOGUE KNOLL

TREES, SHRUBS, AND VINES

Acer saccharinum dasycarpum
[*Acer saccharinum*], Silver maple

Magnolia denudata [*Magnolia heptapeta*],
Yulan magnolia

Prunus cerasus, Sour cherry

Buxus sempervirens, Common box

Buxus sempervirens 'Suffruticosa',
Edging box

Forsythia intermedia 'Spectabilis', Showy
border forsythia

Hibiscus syriacus, Rose-of-Sharon

Lonicera japonica, Japanese honeysuckle

Lycium halimifolium,
Common matrimony vine

Rosa sp., Roses

Rosa centifolia, Cabbage rose

Rosa eglanteria [*Rosa rubiginosa*],
Eglantine rose

Rosa foetida 'Persiana',
Persian yellow rose

Rosa harisonii, Harison's yellow rose

Rosa hugonis, Father Hugo rose

Rosa rugosa, Japanese rose

Rosa spinosissima, Scotch rose

Rosa spinosissima altaica, Altai rose

PERENNIALS

Convallaria majalis, Lily-of-the-valley

Lilium sp., Lily

Paeonia albiflora [*Paeonia lactiflora*],
Chinese peony

Verbascum sp., Mullein

Viola sp., Violet

Cherry Hill, North and West of the Frameyard

This diverse grouping of cherries provides a stunning spring display, more intricate than other local cherry plantings owing to the mixture *Prunus × yedoensis* 'Akebono', *P. sargentii*, *P.* 'Okame', *P. subhirtella* 'Autumnalis', and *P. serotina*, each overlapping their bloom times and providing nuanced hues of pink and white as their blossoms fall like snow in April. Some of the original Sargent cherries are still present, and the diversity in ages of the cherries speaks to the constant renewal and replanting that gardeners undertake to ensure that the cherries will always hold watch over this hillside.

The view into what is now Dumbarton Oaks Park allows one to imagine those wild gardens as a continuation of a cohesive landscape, with formality giving way to nature. Study is underway to consider adding native plants along the fence line as a means of softening the fence and blending the edges of Cherry Hill with the landscape below.

—JK

THE NORTH SLOPE OF THIS KNOLL HAS BEEN PLANTED TO CERTAIN SORTS, mainly, of the single-flowered Japanese Cherries. It is purposely isolated from the rest of the plantations so that the area may be devoted to a display beautiful at one specific time of year and yet not a conspicuous part of the design in constant view. The Cherry trees have done well in this position, but they are unlikely to be long lived. Therefore, provision should be made for renewing this plantation approximately every fifteen or twenty years. The species, such as *Prunus yedoensis* (Japanese name: Yoshino), are probably incorrectly named here, and the names should be determined by some specialist in Prunus. This is equally true of the tree labeled *Kofugen*, which is one of the named varieties of *Prunus serrulata sachalinensis*. The tree labeled *Prunus Sargentii* is also probably a variety of *Prunus serrulata sachalinensis*. The lovely autumn-flowering *Prunus subhirtella autumnalis* is, as its name implies, a variety of one of the most lovely of the Japanese species. This is a slender, graceful tree with small pink flowers. The tree blooms sparsely in the autumn and again in the spring. The tree marked *Prunus shigan* on the Crabapple Hill plant list is probably *Prunus subhirtella*, of which one of the Japanese names is *Shidare-higan-Zakura*. The best trees to add to this plantation when the present trees fail are the species such as *subhirtella*

Looking north from the frameyard toward Cherry Hill, 2009. Photograph by Joe Mills.

Looking northeast toward Cherry Hill from the Ellipse, ca. 1945. LA-GP-9-4, Garden Archives, Dumbarton Oaks, Trustees for Harvard University.

and *serrulata*, rather than the types of double-flowering cherries such as the variety of *serrulata* known as James H. Veitch. These are plants of very short life, and as their flowers are carried in thick, almost artificial, rose-like bunches, they are less easy to adapt to a naturalistic hillside plantation such as this should continue to be. It is therefore suggested that the species *serrulata* and *subhirtella* be made the principal sorts for the group, with the possible additions of *Prunus lannesiana*, *yedoensis*, and *incisa*.

The climate of Washington is rather too hot and dry to permit the adult development of the Japanese Cherries. Therefore they must be considered as plants which require renewal every fifteen to twenty-five years.

Cherry Hill and Kitchen Garden, seen from the balcony at Arbor Terrace, 2021. Note Farrand's use of symmetry and asymmetry for the shed rooflines. Photograph by Sandy Kavalier.

Before the Iris rot, and borer, destroyed the beds of bearded Iris which were formerly planted under the Cherry trees, they made a lovely display, as they bloomed at the same time as the later Cherry blossoms, but the care of the Iris beds proved such a heavy charge in upkeep that they were eliminated, since the Iris had to be constantly weeded, and required division and replanting every three or four years. If, however, the Iris planting can at some future time be renewed, the colors which seemed becoming to the Cherry blossoms were chosen from pale yellows, the whites, and the lavenders, with one or two of the dark purples and deep-maroon reds. The golden yellows and the pinks were avoided, as they did not seem happy in combination with the Cherry flowers.

PLANT LIST: CHERRY HILL, NORTH AND WEST OF THE FRAMEYARD

ON THE SLOPE AT BOTH SIDES OF THE WALK

Prunus sargentii, Sargent cherry

Prunus serrulata sachalinensis,
   Japanese flowering cherry

Prunus serrulata sachalinensis 'Kofugen'

Prunus subhirtella, Higan cherry

Prunus subhirtella 'Autumnalis',
   Autumn-flowering cherry

Prunus subhirtella 'Shidare-Higan-Zakura',
   Flowering cherry

Prunus yedoensis, Yoshino cherry

ALONG THE PATH FROM THE FORSYTHIA BORDER

Kalmia latifolia, Mountain laurel

Azalea nudiflora [*Rhododendron
   periclymenoides*],
   Purple honeysuckle

Hibiscus syriacus, Rose-of-Sharon

Ligustrum amurense, Amur privet

Syringa vulgaris, Common lilac

Vaccinium corymbosum,
   Highbush blueberry

Viburnum dilatatum, Linden viburnum

Viburnum lentago, Sweet viburnum

Viburnum wrightii, Leatherleaf viburnum

GROUND COVERS ALONG THE PATH

Lonicera japonica, Japanese honeysuckle

Vinca minor, Periwinkle

Viola sp., Violet

ON THE FRAMEYARD FENCE

Lonicera sp., Honeysuckle

On the north side of the walk leading from the Cherry Hill toward the Forsythia steps, a varied group of shrubs was planted for the purpose of giving interest to this walk at times of the year when the Cherries were not in bloom. One or two of the common Lilac were planted near the Cherries, as they harmonized in color with the trees, and Rose-of-Sharon (*Hibiscus syriacus*) were added for late-summer effect. *Viburnum dilatatum*, *wrightii*, and *lentago*, and *Vaccinium corymbosum* were set out to give color in autumn, and *Ligustrum amurense* for its late-autumn berries. A few plants of *Kalmia* connected this plantation with the Laurel plantations which stretch below the present division line between Dumbarton Oaks and Dumbarton Oaks Park. There are also groups of *Vinca minor* as under-carpeting to these shrubs, and an occasional *Azalea nudiflora*, combined with ferns and wild Violets as a continuation of the Dumbarton Oaks Park planting. The fence dividing the two units is mainly covered with *Lonicera japonica* which must not be allowed to run riot among the shrubs.

The slope on either side of the steps that rise west of the frameyard has been planted in order to give contrast to the Cherry Hill and to be of interest mainly in winter and early spring. Therefore, the evergreen Barberries, such as

PLANT LIST: THE STEPS WEST OF THE FRAMEYARD
AND NORTH OF THE BIRD WALK

TREES, SHRUBS, AND VINES

Acer dasycarpum [*Acer saccharinum*],
  Silver maple
Magnolia conspicua denudata [*Magnolia
  heptapeta*], Yulan magnolia
Prunus avium, Bird cherry
Prunus cerasus, Sour cherry
Prunus domestica, Common plum
Taxus baccata 'Repandens',
  Spreading English yew
Taxus cuspidata 'Capitata',
  Upright Japanese yew
Buxus sempervirens, Common box
Berberis darwinii, Darwin's barberry
Berberis julianae, Wintergreen barberry
Berberis sargentiana, Sargent barberry
Berberis thunbergii, Japanese barberry
Berberis verruculosa, Warty barberry
Berberis vulgaris, Common barberry
Cotoneaster dielsianus, Diels' cotoneaster
Cotoneaster horizontalis,
  Rock cotoneaster

Jasminum nudiflorum, Winter jasmine
Lonicera fragrantissima,
  Winter honeysuckle
Lonicera nitida, Box honeysuckle
Lonicera sempervirens,
  Trumpet honeysuckle
Lonicera tatarica, Tatarian honeysuckle
Pyracantha coccinea 'Lalandei',
  Leland's fire thorn
Rosa eglanteria [*Rosa rubiginosa*],
  Eglantine rose
Rosa harisonii, Harison's yellow rose
Rosa hugonis, Father Hugo rose
Rosa 'William A. Richardson'
Spiraea prunifolia, Bridal Wreath
Symphoricarpos racemosus
  [*Symphoricarpos albus*],
  Snowberry
Symphoricarpos vulgaris
  [*Symphoricarpos orbiculatus*],
  Indian currant

GROUND COVERS AND SPRING BULBS

Convallaria majalis, Lily-of-the-valley
Muscari botryoides, Grape hyacinth

Scilla siberica, Siberian squill
Viola sp., Violet

---

verruculosa, Sargentiana, Julianae, and *Darwinii,* make the main group, with only vulgaris and *Thunbergii* chosen from the deciduous sorts. The ground cover under these Barberries is made of *Scilla siberica, Muscari botryoides,* Lily-of-the-valley (*Convallaria majalis*) and Violets. The autumn-fruiting Snowberry and Indian Currant are also used, as they are neither of them tall-growing shrubs and they have interesting autumn fruit. It is important to keep the shrubs on either side of the steps of fairly small type, as tall-growing material which would reach a height of six or eight feet would dwarf the steps and unpleasantly narrow the view to the northern hillside. The flat-growing *Cotoneaster horizontalis,* and *Lonicera nitida* and *sempervirens* make this walk and these steps agreeable even in late autumn or winter. A few of the winter-flowering Honeysuckle (*Lonicera fragrantissima*)

Cherry Hill, looking east, 2009. Photograph by Joe Mills.

and a few plants of the winter-flowering Jasmine (*Jasminum nudiflorum*) make this walk, which would otherwise be of little interest in early spring, attractive through the year.

A few of the Roses from the hill north of the ellipse border the step plantation. They are principally chosen from the yellows, like William Allen Richardson, *Hugonis*, and Harison's Yellow. One plant of *Magnolia denudata* and two or three different sorts of the European Cherries, such as *avium*, *domestica*, and *Cerasus*, bridge the group to the Japanese kinds on the hillside below.

It is not thought important to add or keep shrubs of temporary spring interest, such as *Spiraea prunifolia*, but a few shrub-trained *Pyracantha coccinea Lalandei* will add to the winter-berry effect.

The Steps from the Kitchen Garden to the Lilac Circle, the Lovers' Lane Trellis, and the Fence

Farrand briefly mentions the frameyard to help orient the reader, but this space is no longer extant in its original conception as a collection of cold frames and a pithouse-style greenhouse. However, the area lives on as a nursery housing rare or hard-to-find trees. Replacements for the *Prunus × blireiana* that shade Plum Walk were planted here in 2020 after a multi-year search and will be trained as replacements for the Plum Walk allée.

The highlight of this section is the charming sunny opening with a surrounding shady border now known as Camellia Circle (formerly the Lilac Circle), since the lilacs were replaced due to insufficient light conditions. Visitors are greeted by this oasis of light after emerging from the deep shade of the Grape Arbor and descending the curved steps through the now mature trifoliate orange. Fall-blooming *Camellia sasanqua* 'Setsugekka' and spring blooming *Viburnum × burkwoodii* comprise the backbone and are ensconced in a woodland-inspired border. The circle of turf in the center contains spring bulbs, including *Narcissus Cammasia, Ipheion*, and *Puschkinia libanotica*, adding early spring interested to this multi-season garden. —JK

ON THE NORTH SIDE OF THE KITCHEN GARDEN LIES THE FRAMEYARD AND working area which supplies most of the plants for the Kitchen Garden and the terraces. This is divided from the Kitchen Garden by the English-Oak-paling fence, which was imported in the days when this was possible. The hand-rifted Oak paling has weathered to a pleasant color, and, as the south side of the paling is sheltered, several sorts of climbing Roses—the Silver Moon is one—have been set out, where they thrive. As the walk and steps leave the north end of the Grape Arbor and turn down the steep hill, they are surrounded by Lilacs, *Ligustrum ovalifolium* and *amurense*, and a few of the Rose-of-Sharon. The ground carpet among these shrubs is of Lily-of-the-valley, Grape Hyacinths, and Forget-me-not. And, as one approaches the circle, the Hardy Orange (*Poncirus*) makes a group on the north side of the walk balancing that on the south side. There are also a few Osage Orange (*Maclura pomifera*), and some of the Silver Maples (*Acer saccharinum*) from the north end of Melisande's Allée close the space between the walk and the allée itself.

The Cutting Garden with the Kitchen Garden and Grape Arbor in the background, past the allée of *Prunus × blireiana*, 2021. Photograph by Sandy Kavalier.

PLANT LIST: THE STEPS FROM THE KITCHEN GARDEN EASTWARD TO THE LOVERS' LANE FENCE, PAST AND INCLUDING THE LILAC CIRCLE

TREES, SHRUBS, AND VINES

Acer saccharinum, Silver maple
Juglans nigra, Black walnut
Liriodendron tulipifera, Tulip poplar
Hibiscus syriacus, Rose-of-Sharon
Ligustrum amurense, Amur privet
Ligustrum ovalifolium, California privet
Lonicera fragrantissima,
    Winter honeysuckle

Maclura pomifera, Osage orange
Philadelphus coronarius, Mock orange
Philadelphus grandiflorus [*Philadelphus
    inodorus grandiflorus*]
Poncirus trifoliata, Trifoliate orange
Syringa vulgaris, Common lilac

PERENNIALS AND SPRING BULBS

Convallaria majalis, Lily-of-the-valley
Hemerocallis flava, [*Hemerocallis
    lilioasphodelus*], Yellow daylily
Muscari sp., Grape hyacinth

Myosotis scorpioides, Forget-me-not
Scilla campanulata [*Endymion
    hispanicus*], Spanish bluebell
Scilla siberica, Siberian scilla

ON THE NORTH FENCE

Rosa 'Silver moon'
Rosa 'Mermaid'

ON THE BOARD FENCE

Jasminum nudiflorum, Winter jasmine

Poncirus trifoliata, trifoliate orange. Photograph by Sandy Kavalier.

The Camellia Circle, looking south toward the lower allée, 2021. Photograph by Sandy Kavalier.

The circle originally was planted to a row of Lilacs, but these did not survive in the somewhat shady positions given them, and they were therefore replaced by *Philadelphus coronarius* and *grandiflorus* which make a double hedge around the little circle, in the middle of which there is a carpet of Lily-of-the-valley with an outer border of the early-flowering Day Lily (*Hemerocallis flava*). A few Forget-me-nots and some Grape Hyacinths stray into this carpet and are not unwelcome.

As the steps pass the circle and drop down the hill toward the north end of Melisande's Allée, they should be bordered with Ivy and Lily-of-the-valley. The little perspective, with its polychrome decoration, makes the end of the walk at the Lovers' Lane wall and fence. Old Osage Orange and Privet screen the ends to the little perspective and give it a frame. A few plants of the early-flowering Honeysuckle (*Lonicera fragrantissima*) give scent in the early spring, at the time some of the first bulbs are in flower.

The North End of Melisande's Allée, Below the Change of Level

This section of garden serves to visually elongate Mélisande's Allée from above and to screen activity along Lovers' Lane from below. While the bench still anchors the prospect at the grade change, the easternmost steps curving around the retaining wall have been lost to the encroaching understory. This set of steps will be reinstalled following a restoration of the screening plantings, currently underway.   —JK

WHERE THE UPPER LEVEL OF MELISANDE'S ALLÉE ENDS, A SHARP BREAK is inevitable, but the curving steps leading to the lower level around the slightly curved wall should be invisible from the upper side, out of sight until the break in level is within a few feet.

The seat following the curve of the wall is enclosed by the two curving flights of steps. This seat looks north over the north end of the allée which, although bordered by the same Maple trees, is slightly different in character from the upper level of the walk. Under the Maple trees in this lower section there are also Privets (*Ligustrum ovalifolium*) and a few of the old Osage Orange (*Maclura pomifera*) which were a part of the original planting of Dumbarton.

The Grape Arbor marks the western boundary to this end of the walk, and the steep bank separating it is planted to Lilacs, with a ground cover of Lily-of-the-valley and Narcissus in spring.

There are also wild Violets, *Scilla*, and *Muscari* on either side of the walk, but no plantation massive in size or in foliage would be appropriate in this position. One or two fine Tulip trees (*Liriodendron tulipifera*) may be mixed in with the Maples between the walk and the Lovers' Lane wall. And, as Melisande's Allée ends in the walk leading from the Lilac Circle to the little artificial perspective southeast of it, there are groups of *Poncirus trifoliata* (the Hardy Orange) which is useful for the delicious fragrance of its flowers and for the picturesque and thorny growth of orange-like fruit in the autumn. There are one or two Black Walnuts (*Juglans nigra*), but these are not an essential part of the picture and might well be replaced by Tulip trees when the Walnuts are no longer attractive.

Farrand-designed bench at the transition from Mélisande's Allée to the lower allée, 1978. LA-GP-31-8, Garden Archives, Dumbarton Oaks, Trustees for Harvard University.

PLANT LIST: THE LOWER LEVEL OF MELISANDE'S ALLÉE

TREES AND SHRUBS

Citrus trifoliata [*Poncirus trifoliata*], Trifoliate orange
Juglans nigra, Black walnut
Liriodendron tulipifera, Tulip poplar

Ligustrum ovalifolium, California privet
Maclura pomifera, Osage orange
Syringa vulgaris, Common lilac

PERENNIALS AND SPRING BULBS

Convallaria majalis, Lily-of-the-valley
Muscari sp., Grape hyacinth
Narcissus sp., Daffodil

Scilla sp., Squill
Viola sp., Wild violet

The lower allée with *Scilla siberica* in full bloom, 2021. Photograph by Sandy Kavalier.

The Upper Level of Mélisande's Allée

Many of the original silver maples retain their positions, even though the eastern row has been obscured by the understory, as is the case in the lower allée. In fact, the allée itself is in a state of flux, as silver maple replacements have been made using disease resistant American elm varieties (*Ulmus* × 'Pioneer' and more recently *Ulmus americana* 'Jefferson'), which provide similar majestic architecture but are superior in structure and robustness to the storm-damage prone silver maples.

A diverse mix of spring bulbs, including *Narcissus*, *Scilla*, *Mertensia*, *Crocus*, *Eranthis*, *Erythronium*, *Galanthus*, and *Leucojum*, leap forth each spring and reward visitors with a parade of ephemerals before giving way to turf grass in the summer.

The brick walk retains its role as it dances through this planting. This path was lifted and reset in 2017–18 as part of a stormwater project that placed a main water supply line beneath the walkway—it being the farthest spot from adjacent trees—in order to protect the allée.   —JK

THIS LONG, SLOPING AVENUE OF OLD SILVER MAPLE TREES MAKES THE background to the Lovers' Lane Pool, and should always be kept in as good condition as physically and financially possible, as it is an essential part of the composition of the pool and adds much to its quiet charm. The allée is thirty-five feet wide, with Silver Maples planted on either side, starting north of the pool and stretching down to the break in the level, close to the east end of the Herbaceous Border. These trees, and the avenue between them, not only give distance and perspective to the pool, but they act as barriers to separate this whole unit from the boundary wall just inside of Lovers' Lane and from the Herb Garden and Orchard and Herbaceous Border to the west. Where old trees fail in this avenue, they should be replaced by trees, if possible, ten to twelve inches in diameter, as small trees of puny girth would change the whole effect of the long lines of arching branches. This particular sort of white Maple (*Acer saccharinum*) should be used, and not one of its varieties.

The ground carpet between the trees should be mainly Vinca minor, but if this proves difficult to keep free of disease, sheared Japanese Honeysuckle (*Lonicera*

The western line of Mélisande's Allée and transition to the Orchard, 2021. Photograph by Sandy Kavalier.

japonica) may be grown, although this does not cling as close to the ground and therefore has a tendency to become too fuzzy for this particular neighborhood.

Spring bulbs, such as *Crocus*, *Chionodoxa*, and *Scilla sibirica*, Lily-of-the-valley, and perhaps an occasional group of the poet's *Narcissus* or the Jonquil (*Narcissus jonquilla simplex*) may be planted in the ground cover.

Wild Violets and Forget-me-nots, and an occasional clump of Iris, may also be used. And on either side of the avenue of trees, little groups of Spice-bush (*Benzoin aestivale*) and the three Privets (*Ligustrum japonicum*, *vulgare*, and *amurense*) may be used as low screens to hide the east boundary and the gardens to the west.

Also, a few Japanese Maples (*Acer palmatum*) have been used. And, at the foot of the Herbaceous Border between the north end of the allée and the east end of the border, a Norway Maple (or is it a Sycamore Maple?), *Acer platanoides*, stands behind one of the big Irish Yews. This tree is interesting neither in its foliage nor its type, so, when it can be replaced by another tree, perhaps another Silver Maple, or a Sugar Maple, would be a change for the better.

The brick walk leading down the allée is really too narrow for convenience in walking. It is, however, necessary to keep this walk narrow in order not to dwarf the scale of the width of the allée and the height of the trees. The position for the walk was decided on after many stakings, much thought, and many changes, and its width was reluctantly determined upon when it was seen that a four or five-foot walk changed the whole scale of the allée so that it was a tree-bordered walk, rather than an arch of trees under which a narrow path winds its way.

PLANT LIST: THE UPPER LEVEL OF MELISANDE'S ALLÉE

TREES AND SHRUBS

Acer palmatum, Japanese maple
Acer platanoides, Norway maple
Acer saccharinum, Silver maple
Liriodendron tulipifera, Tulip poplar
Benzoin aestivale [*Lindera benzoin*], Spicebush

Jasminum nudiflorum, Winter jasmine
Ligustrum amurense, Amur privet
Ligustrum japonicum, Wax-leaf privet
Ligustrum vulgare, Common privet

GROUND COVER, PERENNIALS, AND SPRING BULBS

Chionodoxa sp., Glory-of-the-snow
Convallaria majalis, Lily-of-the-valley
Crocus sp., Crocus
Iris sp., Flag

Myosotis scorpioides, Forget-me-not
Narcissus sp., Daffodil
Vinca minor, Periwinkle
Viola sp., Wild violet

The Lovers' Lane Screen Plantations

The Lovers' Lane Pool, as originally designed, included several invasive plants, as did many garden areas. In a multi-year project, we are reevaluating the entire landscape, starting with this area, to improve the ecosystem services and to replace invasive plants with more appropriate species. The buffer planting here had become overrun with invasive plants such as privet (*Ligustrum* sp.), porcelain vine (*Ampelopsis brevipedunculata*), and honeysuckle (*Lonicera japonica*), and the undergrowth had encroached upon the eastern line of the allée. Due to the narrowness of the screening buffer between the allée and the property edge, we implemented a phased approach. First, some invasive plants were removed from behind the allée to open planting space and to introduce light. Then, in spring 2020, gardeners planted 150 native shrubs, including *Lindera benzoin, Cephalanthus occidentalis, Ilex verticillata, Itea virginica,* and *Viburnum dentatum.* These shrubs were selected for their native status and ornamental characteristics that make them fitting additions to Farrand's plant palette. As these natives mature, the remaining invasive plants (now providing privacy from the lane below) will be completely removed, restoring the eastern allée line. —JK

FROM R STREET TO THE BOUNDARY OF DUMBARTON OAKS PARK, A STONE wall protects the Dumbarton Oaks property from intrusion. Inside this wall, a thick screen of mainly deciduous material should be kept constantly replaced and in good condition. On the south end of the boundary, an area of about one hundred yards in length should have, in addition to the deciduous material, some evergreen plants, such as Holly, Hemlock, and Box, added to the taller growing shrubs. Houses can be seen from the south front of Dumbarton Oaks behind the south end of the Lovers' Lane boundary, and therefore the evergreens are essential in this part of the border.

Montrose Park protects Dumbarton Oaks on the main length of its eastern boundary, so screen plant material may be deciduous from approximately one hundred yards north of the R Street and Lovers' Lane corner. This part of the bank should be planted with deciduous trees harmonizing both with those in Melisande's Allée and with the trees on the east side of Lovers' Lane, in the park itself. Undoubtedly, replacement of the Silver Maples in Melisande's Allée will be necessary from time to time, as these trees are not as long-lived as the great White

Lovers' Lane path, looking south up Mélisande's Allée toward Lover's Lane Pool, 1965–70. LA-GP-31-11, Garden Archives, Dumbarton Oaks, Trustees for Harvard University.

Oaks. Melisande's Allée has seemed lovely in its delicate fringe of Silver Maple, and it is hard to think of any other tree which would give this soft and graceful frame to the long green walk.

The description of the Melisande's Allée planting is made at this point in order to indicate the type of tree which will harmonize with the allée planting. In certain places where the park boundary of heavy trees comes close to Lovers' Lane, the boundary trees on the Dumbarton Oaks land are less important than tall shrubs, which can fill the space between the Silver-Maple allée and the top of the Lovers' Lane wall. The common Privet (*Ligustrum ovaltfolium*), Virginia Creeper on the fence, and an occasional Dogwood or Spicebush (*Benzoin aestivale*)[2] will probably give sufficient variety for this planting, which should not be so conspicuous in its makeup as to draw attention from the main perspective of the allée.

2   *Hortus* Third: *Lindera benzoin*

The poet's daffodil, *Narcissus poeticus* 'Pheasant Eye'.
Photograph by Sandy Kavalier.

As Lovers' Lane lies far below the level of most of the adjoining Dumbarton land, a high wall has been built to retain the upper levels. At the top of this big retaining wall on the west side of Lovers' Lane, a split chestnut French fence was placed, and, as it is thought not unlikely that before long this fence may need replacement and repair, it is suggested that the Habitant-type of cedar poles, of the same height as the split chestnut, should be used for replacement. The cedar poles will be more permanent than the split chestnut, and although their first cost will be higher than the DuBois French fencing when it was bought, the cedar is recommended, as it is sturdier and of longer life.

The fence and wall should be covered with hanging masses of white Clematis, Honeysuckle, Virginia Creeper, and Ivy; and fence and wall should make one unit as seen from below in Lovers' Lane. Thanks to the festooning of the planting, the wall is not objectionable, although it is high and rigid.

The Lovers' Lane Pool

The Lovers' Lane Pool and surrounding garden has the air of an ancient place uncovered rather than built, and conservation efforts have been carefully planned to preserve this feeling of timelessness. Similar invasive plant removals have led to the replacement of honeysuckle (*Lonicera japonica*) on the slope with winter jasmine (*Jasmine nudiflorum*), though the bamboo (*Pseudosassa japonica*) between the columns remains. The stormwater project of 2018 also retrofitted the fountains at Fountain Terrace and Lovers' Lane Pool into recirculating systems. This, along with an additional project to install ultraviolet filters, has served to reduce the water usage both in running and cleaning the fountains. The columns and urns were restored in 2021, beginning a period of renewed focus on ornament conservation across the gardens as they pass their centennial.

—JK

IT WILL DOUBTLESS BE REALIZED BY THOSE STANDING AT THE EDGE OF Lovers' Lane Pool that the change in level from the steps opposite the orangery to the pool itself amounts to a very considerable number of feet—approximately 55. The whole arrangement surrounding the Lovers' Lane Pool is, again, entirely controlled by the natural slopes of the ground and the desire to keep as many of the native trees as possible unhurt and undisturbed. The big Walnut at the south end of the pool has been gracefully framed by the surrounding levels, and the pool itself so placed that it does not interfere with the roots of either the big Silver Maple (*Acer saccharinum*) to the north of the pool or the boundary trees to the east.

The Lovers' Lane Pool and the seats surrounding its south end were never intended for a large audience; probably at most fifty people could be comfortably seated. These seats have been adapted from the well-known open-air theatre on the slopes of the Janiculum Hill at the Accademia degli Arcadi Bosco Parrasio. The shape of the theatre at Dumbarton was copied from the one in Rome, but the slopes surrounding the Dumbarton theatre are far steeper than those on the Italian hillsides and therefore the seats are considerably raised from one level to another. In order to give seclusion to this little theatre, it has been surrounded by cast-stone columns, also baroque in design and taken in their essential ideas

Lovers' Lane Pool, looking north down Mélisande's Allée, 2010.
Photograph by Alexandre Tokovinine.

Farrand specified that the brick and ornament should be allowed to become lichen and moss covered, 2021. Photograph by Sandy Kavalier.

Above: Lovers' Lane Pool, 1967. LA-GP-29-12, Garden Archives, Dumbarton Oaks, Trustees for Harvard University.

Below: Pan sculpture, by Francis Minturn Sedgwick, conceived and designed by Beatrix Farrand. Photograph by Sandy Kavalier.

PLANT LIST: LOVERS' LANE POOL

TREES, SHRUBS, AND VINES SURROUNDING THE POOL

Tsuga canadensis, Canadian hemlock

Acer saccharinum, Silver maple

Fagus sylvatica 'Purpurea'
    [*Fagus sylvatica* 'Atropunicea'],
    European purple-leaved beech

Juglans regia, Persian walnut

Liriodendron tulipifera, Tulip poplar

Prunus sp., Cherry

Salix babylonica, Weeping willow

Buxus sempervirens 'Suffruticosa',
    Edging box

Ligustrum amurense, Amur privet

Ligustrum japonicum, Wax-leaf privet

Lonicera japonica, Japanese honeysuckle

Bambusa sp., Bamboo

ON THE TRELLIS

Hedera sp., Ivy

Jasminum sp., Jasmine

Lonicera sp., Honeysuckle

Pueraria lobata, Kudzu vine

ON THE BRICK WALL

Vinca minor, Periwinkle

GROUND COVER, PERENNIALS, AND SPRING BULBS AROUND THE POOL

Crocus sp., Crocus

Vinca minor, Periwinkle

Viola sp., Violet

SPRING BULBS AND PERENNIALS UNDERNEATH THE BEECH TREE

Crocus sp., Crocus

Eranthis hyemalis, Winter aconite

Erythronium sp., Dog-tooth violet

Fritillaria sp., Guinea-hen flower

Galanthus nivalis, Common snowdrop

Hepatica sp., Liverleaf

Narcissus sp., Daffodil

Osmorhiza sp., Sweet cicely

Podophyllum peltatum, Mayapple

Trillium sp., Trillium

Triteleia sp., Triteleia

Viola sp., Violet

TREES AND SHRUBS ON THE BANK OUTSIDE THE EAST WALL OF THE FOUNTAIN TERRACE

Acer saccharinum, Silver maple

Crataegus cordata
    [*Crataegus phaenopyrum*],
    Washington thorn

Platanus occidentalis, Buttonwood

Pyrus lecontei 'Kieffer', Kieffer pear

Buxus sempervirens, Common box

Cydonia sinensis, Chinese quince

Jasminum nudiflorum, Winter jasmine

Ligustrum amurense, Amur privet

Lovers' Lane Pool, looking south from the top of Mélisande's Allée, 2021.
Photograph by Sandy Kavalier.

from Italian gardens of the baroque period. The cast-stone columns are connected with a split natural-wood lattice in long horizontal rectangles. These trellises are covered by both deciduous and evergreen creepers, such as Honeysuckle, Ivy, and Jasmine; and on the east trellis, where protection is needed from the very close easterly boundary, the heavy-growing Kudzu has been amply used. The ground cover under the seats is of *Vinca minor* and this also surrounds the pool. The Lovers' Lane Pool was designed in its outline to give added perspective to the length available, to act as a sounding board for those using the small stage at the north end of the pool, as well as to act as a reflecting mirror to the overhanging Silver Maples on the north.

Outside the trellis, it is protected by some few plants of Privet, both the Japanese and *amurense*, and a few plants of Bamboo; and, on the west side of the pool, a Weeping Willow breaks the steep slope of the bank north of where the seats end.

The Orchard

The Japanese pagoda tree (*Sophora japonica*) was struck by lightning in the early 2000s and was removed, but not before being replaced with another Sophora from a nearby location that has now developed a confident presence at the top of the Orchard hill. The Orchard now contains varieties of sour cherry, peach, plum, apple, persimmon, Chinese quince, and, of course, apple trees.   —JK

THE NORTH SLOPE OF THIS HILL IS PLANTED MAINLY TO APPLES, TO GIVE variety though not especially chosen for the perfection of their fruit. These apples should be more carefully cultivated for fruit in the future than they have been in the past, as they were originally planted as a feature in the landscape rather than as an item of food production. The old trees, as they deteriorate, should be replaced by those of better fruit-quality, as the importance of the fruit supply to Dumbarton Oaks as a part of Harvard is more important than the fruit supply to a private house. The study of which variety should be chosen for this purpose should be carefully gone into, as winter-keeping apples are more important to provide for the students and staff than those which ripen in the early season. Some Crabapples are desirable to keep, not only for the beauty of their bloom in spring but also because the jelly from their fruit is always welcome. A few Pears have been planted at the top of the Orchard hill, forming a hedge around the Herb and Fountain Terraces on the north and east sides—Kieffer only.

Crataegus cordata is added to the Orchard, but may be eliminated when it can be replaced with better fruit trees. One or two Red Maples may also be eliminated, and further fruit trees added, but the big *Sophora japonica* is so lovely a part of the mid-summer scene that it should be kept in its position, or replaced; its summer flower and the grace of its pinnate foliage is most valuable as a part of this composition.

On the path leading from the north gate of the Rose Garden to the Herbaceous Border, down the steep hill, a few shrubs have been planted to edge the path and give it spring flower. A Weigela, the sweet-scented *Philadelphus coronarius*, *Prunus glandulosa*, and, for spring flower, one or two tufts of the

The Orchard, looking west, 2021. Photograph by Sandy Kavalier.

211

The Orchard, looking northeast, ca. 1975. LA-GP-21-7, Garden Archives, Dumbarton Oaks, Trustees for Harvard University.

early-flowering Jasmine (*Jasminum nudiflorum*) with an occasional bunch of Yellowroot (*Zanthorhiza apiifolia*).

Also close to the steps there are Violets of different sorts, which may be added to in their variety, as some of the white Violets (*Viola cucullata alba*) might grow well in this climate and would add a change of color which would be both welcome and attractive.

PLANT LIST: ORCHARD HILL

ON THE SLOPE

Acer rubrum, Red maple
Crataegus cordata [*Crataegus phaenopyrum*], Washington thorn

Malus sp., Apple and Crabapple
Pyrus lecontei 'Kieffer', Kieffer pear
Sophora japonica, Japanese pagoda tree

ALONG THE PATH TO THE HERBACEOUS BORDER

Prunus glandulosa, Flowering almond
Philadelphus coronarius, Mock orange
Jasminum nudiflorum, Winter jasmine

Weigela sp., Weigela
Zanthorhiza apiifolia [*Xanthorhiza simplicissima*], Shrub yellowroot

GROUND COVERS

Ampelopsis quinquefolia [*Parthenocissus quinquefolia*], Woodbine

Viola sp., Violet

Prunus × *blireiana*, among the first signs of spring. Photograph by Sandy Kavalier.

The Goat Trail and the Steps to the Herbaceous Border

Masses of rockspray cotoneaster (*Cotoneaster horizontalis*) north of the Rose Garden and mock orange (*Philadelphus* sp.) along the curving steps from arbor terrace are effective in softening the grades. The bench and arbor along the path are original, and plans for their reproduction are underway as the next phase of a comprehensive project, which resulted in the creation of three-dimensional technical models of twenty-eight pieces of Farrand-designed furniture. These models will greatly aid in the reproduction of other historical pieces, as the Farrand-designed furniture is an important component of her kinesthetic vision for the gardens and landscape. The actual utility walk referenced by Farrand is no longer extant, as the surrounding plantings have filled the space. The steps and path are now colloquially called the Goat Trail.   —JK

THIS UTILITY WALK, LEADING FROM THE NORTH END OF THE BOX TERRACE to the Herb Garden, is planted on the north with an occasional shrub (*Weigela*), on the west end with an occasional *Philadelphus*. Between the flagstone steps and the retaining, garden walls, spring bulbs, such as *Scilla nutans* and *Narcissus*, make an attractive border. The early-flowering Jasmine is planted on the outside of some of the walls, and north of the walk a small fence of paling is covered with lighter sorts of *Clematis*, such as *texensis*, *Jackmanii*, and *virginiana*. *Phlox subulata* is also planted between the walk and the garden walls. And, at the west end, one or two bushes of Box tie this planting into the planting of the Box Walk.

As many Jasmines as possible may be used as frames to the steps leading from the Goat Trail to the Herbaceous Border, combined with Honeysuckle. And on either side of the steps, masses of bulbs should be planted, under the fruit trees and fairly close to the walk, so that they can be seen by those using this steep but convenient communication.

Though the original Goat Trail no longer exists, this path and the associated steps through the Orchard have assumed that name, 2021. Photograph by Sandy Kavalier.

This original seat and niche, designed by Beatrix Farrand, still sits along atop the Orchard, ca. 1975. LA-GP-21-4, Garden Archives, Dumbarton Oaks, Trustees for Harvard University.

PLANT LIST: THE GOAT TRAIL,
FROM THE WISTERIA ARBOR TO THE BOX WALK

ON OR OVER THE RETAINING WALL OF THE ROSE GARDEN

Jasminum nudiflorum, Winter jasmine   *Rosa* sp., Climbing roses

AT THE FOOT OF THE WALL (EXAMPLES ONLY)

Narcissus sp., Daffodil   *Scilla nutans* [*Endymion nonscriptus*],
Phlox subulata, Mountain phlox   English bluebell

ON THE FENCE ALONG THE NORTH SIDE OF THE TRAIL

Clematis jackmanii, Jackman clematis   *Clematis virginiana*, Virgin's bower
Clematis texensis, Scarlet clematis

ON THE ORCHARD SIDE OF THE FENCE

Philadelphus coronarius, Mock orange   *Weigela* sp., Weigela

AT THE WEST END OF THE TRAIL

Buxus sempervirens, Common box

The Herbaceous Border

The Herbaceous Border, like the Fountain Terrace, may showcase different plant varieties than it did in Farrand's time, but the overall effect of her design is intact. Like at Fountain Terrace, tulips welcome the spring visitor and soon give way to layers of annuals and perennials, predominantly soft pastel pinks, yellows, lavenders, blues, and whites, against the backdrop of the yew hedge. Chrysanthemums are also displayed in the beds, but the colors here are a continuation of the soft summer colors. Early blooming chrysanthemums are used and then replaced with violas and tulip bulbs while the weather conditions are still optimal. Because the tulip bulbs are not removed after blooming, the tulip display here is a mixture of varieties from several years and is much less formal in appearance than the solid blocks of bold color on Fountain Terrace.   —JK

THIS WIDE BORDER LEADING FROM AN UPPER LEVEL, ON WHICH A BIG Irish Yew is planted on a cross terrace, to an Irish Yew at the lower, foot of the border in a Yew enclosure, makes the main planting at Dumbarton Oaks of perennials and early, pink-flowering Tulips and other spring bulbs. The permanent enclosure of this border is one which requires careful study. Yew hedges are, without question, the most pictorially attractive, but twenty-years of experience has proved that their life and growth can hardly be expected to exceed twenty years in the Washington climate. Whether to count on the constant replacement of these Yew hedges, given the annoyance of waiting for the young Yews to grow to sufficient height, or whether to replace the Yew enclosure by a stone wall, and so widen the border and give space to certain rarer shrubs among the herbaceous material, must be considered. The design for this wall has already been made, and while it may seem inadvisable to consider any change as drastic as the change from Yew to stone, it nevertheless should be thoroughly discussed and decided upon, after careful reflection. It would seem, on the whole and from the far distant point of view, wise to consider the wall building as most sensible.

The composition of the planting of the Herbaceous Border should be rather carefully chosen from material which is somewhat unusual in its character and

Looking west, up the Herbaceous Border in the late summer toward "Mrs. Yew," 2021. Photograph by Sandy Kavalier.

A unique perspective looking west at the Herbaceous Border from above in spring, 2021. Photograph by Sandy Kavalier.

The pastel colors of the Herbaceous Border tulips perfectly reflect Farrand's desire to diffentiate this color palette from that of Fountain Terrace, 2021. Photograph by Sandy Kavalier.

harmonious in its color tones. Since the Fountain Terrace has usually been adapted to the orange, yellow, bronze, and maroon shades, it has seemed natural, during the spring and summer months, to give the shades of pink, red, lavender, and pale blue to the range of the Herbaceous Border. Naturally, considerable numbers of annuals must be used to keep the border presentable during the season; and at the end of the summer season a thorough change is made in its planting, and it becomes, for the autumn, a series of groups of Chrysanthemums. Most usually these are chosen in the autumn colors of bronze, yellow, and maroon, as both the pinks and the whites tend to become shabby and muddy looking after the First frost whereas the yellows continue in their beauty until well along in November.

PLANT LIST: THE HERBACEOUS BORDER

Note: The border planting changes with the seasons, from spring-flowering bulbs through chrysanthemums. The permanent surrounding shrubs are listed below, and a representative seed list is given.

THE HEDGE

Taxus cuspidata 'Capitata', Upright Japanese yew

AT THE HEAD AND FOOT OF THE BORDER

Taxus baccata 'Hibernica fastigiata' [*Taxus baccata* 'Stricta'], Irish yew

A PLANT ORDER TO SUTTON AND SONS, 1943

Alcea, Hollyhock 'Brilliant Mixture'
Anchusa 'Sutton's Royal Blue'
Cheiranthus, Wallflower 'Blood Red'
Cheiranthus, Wallflower 'Cloth of Gold'
Chrysanthemum superbum, Shasta daisy
Dianthus barbatus,
    Sweet William 'Pink Beauty'
Dimorphotheca aurantiaca, Cape marigold
Eschscholzia 'Special Mixture'
Gaillardia 'Special Mixture'
Geum 'Mrs. Bradshaw'
Geum 'Lady Stratheden'
Matthiola incana 'Annua',
    Ten weeks stock (delicate pink)
Matthiola incana 'Annua',
    Ten weeks stock (pale mauve)

Matthiola incana 'Annua',
    Ten weeks stock (white)
Petunia 'Blue Bedder'
Phlox drummondi 'Blue Beauty'
Phlox drummondi 'Pink Beauty'
Phlox drummondi 'Sutton's Purity'
Phlox drummondi 'Violet Beauty'
Saponaria vaccaria
    [*Vaccaria pyramidata*], Dairy pink
Scabiosa 'Azure Fairy' (mauve)
Scabiosa 'Black Prince'
Scabiosa 'Cherry Red'
Statice sinuata [*Limonium sinuatum*]
    'Royal Blue'
Statice sinuata [*Limonium sinuatum*]
    'Yellow Bonduelli'
Tagetes, Marigold 'Golden Gem'

The Walk Connecting the Herbaceous Border with the Box Walk

This charming passage, though primarily designed for utility and access around steep grades, provides a magical experience when the path and wall caps are covered in fallen magnolia blossoms. Above, the magnolia reaches over the Box Walk and its simple slope planting, as Farrand suggests. Below, a window to the Cutting Garden, framed by the charming tool shed roof and yew hedge gives way to the Plum Walk (*Prunus × blireiana*) behind.

   While the arbor is long gone, "Mrs. Yew" has achieved a grand scale and the former arbor wall has become a place in which to recognize past garden directors. The whimsical goose weathervane sitting atop the upper tool shed was reproduced in 2017. While original drawings existed, the intended scale of the piece was a mystery until gardeners found a remnant letter "N" in the soil and the scale was able to be determined.   —JK

THIS WALK MAKES A CONNECTION BETWEEN THE NORTH END OF THE BOX Walk and the west end of the Herbaceous Border. The reason it has been designed in this place is because the approach to the Herbaceous Border from the top of the Box Walk would be impossibly steep and implied formidable step building. Therefore the roundabout route has been determined upon, as the end of the Box Walk makes a convenient crossroad from which the Ellipse can be entered on its south side, a service court can be reached on the west, and the Herbaceous Border and vegetable garden may be approached on the east side. A Yew hedge at the upper edge of the Peony beds on either side of the upper, western tool house is eliminated, and is replaced by a low, stone wall which may be overplanted by flowering material, such as some of the smaller Clematises (as *texansis*, or some of the *Viticella* hybrids).

   The steps between the Box Walk and the lower approach walk to the Herbaceous Border are in a very steep bank. This should be rather lightly planted, as looking up to the Box Walk from below will probably be more effective than any flower or shrub grouping.

   In the beds on either side of the western tool house, Peonies are planted, mainly of single sorts, with a ground cover of *Scilla siberica* and some *Phlox subulata*

The charm of this connecting walk is unparalleled when the saucer magnolia is blooming overhead, 2021. Photograph by Sandy Kavalier.

PLANT LIST: THE WALK CONNECTING THE WEST END OF THE HERBACEOUS BORDER TO THE LOWER LEVEL OF THE BOX WALK

TREES, SHRUBS, AND VINES

Prunus avium, Bird cherry

Ulmus americana, American elm

Taxus baccata 'Brevifolia', English yew

Taxus baccata 'Hibernica' [*Taxus baccata* 'Stricta'], Irish yew

Taxus cuspidata 'Capitata', Japanese yew

Cydonia vulgaris [*Cydonia oblonga*], Common quince

Spiraea vanhouttei, Van Houtte spirea

Clematis montana rubens [*Clematis montana* 'Undulata' *rubens*]

Jasminum nudiflorum, Winter jasmine

Lycium halimijolium, Common matrimony vine

Wisteria sinensis, Chinese wisteria

GROUND COVER, PERENNIALS, AND SPRING BULBS

Ampelopsis quinquefolia [*Parthenocissus quinquefolia*], Woodbine

Cerastium sp., Mouse-ear chickweed

Myosotis scorpiodes, Forget-me-not

Paeonia albiflora [*Paeonia lactiflora*], Chinese peony

Phlox subulata, Mountain phlox

Primula sp., Primrose

Scilla siberica, Siberian squill

on the walls. The simpler these two planting plans are kept, the better the effect will be.

Along the grass terrace at the top of the Herbaceous Border, surrounding the majestic Irish Yew which is the main feature of the west end of the border, a stone seat has been gouged into the wall and is covered by a one-sided trellis, which should be kept planted to Wisteria, both white and purple, and the early-flowering *Clematis montana rubens*. As the grades surrounding this arbor are extremely awkward, mask plantings, such as *Jasminum nudiflorum* and big masses of Yew, are necessary to hide these levels as they meet between the Orchard and the end of the arbor. On this terrace, spring flowers, such as *Primula*, *Cerastium*, *Myosotis*, and *Phlox*, may be used as ground covers; and on the wall supporting the arbor, and on the arbor also, there may be used some *Parthenocissus* for its autumn color, but it should not be allowed to invade the Wisteria but rather should weave itself into the other plants in order to give autumn effect.

THE MUSEUM WING AND AREAS NOT GENERALLY OPEN TO THE PUBLIC

The Museum Courtyard

This garden is no longer extant, as the courtyard was transformed into museum exhibition space in 1963.   —JK

THE SMALL SIZE OF THIS COURTYARD MAKES GREAT RESTRAINT necessary in the planting, as no large material would be suited to this enclosure. On the north side, on the wall, a Gardenia, Rose, and purple Wisteria, and English Ivy make the wall cover; and on the south side, in order to give the cooler exposure, *Clematis Henryi* is grown, and possibly *Clematis Nellie Moser* could be added if *Henryi* is found to thrive. *Pyracantha* also will do better on this north exposure. And on each end of the north and south walls, *Ilex crenata* markers may be planted.

The steps leading into the court from the Music Room should always be kept simply planted to small, bunchy groups of *Buxus suffruticosa*. In the middle of the courtyard the space is planted to grass, but in time, if grass is found not to thrive, the fine-leaved Ivy (*conglomerata*) could be used as a ground cover, to match the ground cover between the walk and the building which is made of Violets and English Ivy. The center grass plot is edged with a double row of

The museum courtyard (now Museum Gallery), 1978. LA-GP-32-1, Garden Archives, Dumbarton Oaks, Trustees for Harvard University.

PLANT LIST: THE MUSEUM COURTYARD

IN THE NORTH BEDS AND ON THE NORTH WALL

Wisteria sinensis 'Purpurea', Purple
   Chinese wisteria

Hedera helix, English ivy
Viola sp., Violet

FLANKING THE MUSIC ROOM STEPS AT THE EAST

Buxus sempervirens 'Suffruticosa', Edging box

IN THE SOUTH BEDS AND ON THE SOUTH WALL

Clematis henryi, Henry clematis
Pyracantha coccinea 'Lalandei',
   Leland's fire thorn

Wisteria sp., Wisteria
Hedera helix, English ivy
Viola sp., Wild violet

AT THE WEST, NEAR THE GLASS-ENCLOSED PASSAGEWAY

Jasminum nudiflorum, Winter jasmine
Hedera helix, English ivy

Viola sp., Wild violet

IN EACH CORNER

Ilex crenata, Japanese holly

SURROUNDING THE PLOT OF GRASS IN THE CENTER

Buxus sempervirens 'Suffruticosa', Edging box

Box, ending at the eastern end with two clipped clumps of *Buxus suffruticosa*. The planting of this court must be constantly reviewed so that it does not get out of scale with the charming little buildings which surround it. On the west end of the court, two groups of the early-flowering, winter Jasmine (*Jasminum nudiflorum*) are placed to balance each other; and Wisteria is trained on the architrave which carries a Greek inscription. This courtyard is hardly a garden, but should be thought of more as an unroofed room adjoining the Music Room and the museum; its scale is really an interior and not an outdoor scale, and the planting should be done with this kept constantly in mind.

The Service Entrance at 1701 Thirty-Second Street

The service entrance was removed in 1963 with the addition of the Garden Library.

—JK

THIS IS THE MAIN SERVICE ENTRANCE TO THE WHOLE DUMBARTON OAKS building group: library and living quarters and museum. A good deal of material of fairly large size must be easily distributed from this point. Therefore, planting as little encumbering as possible should be planned for this area. Between this service entrance and the R Street exit gate, a heavy screen of evergreens, such as Hemlocks or *Deodara*, and Sugar Maple and Tulip trees should be kept, as this west boundary is alarmingly open to the city streets and nearby houses. In the actual service enclosure, Ivy on the wooden-lattice fence and Violets in the border below the fence are practically all that are needed, with the exception of a few Ivies on the lines and the connecting link to the museum.

Much of this area gets hard wear, and for this reason choice plants, such as fine Box bushes, are not wise to use, but rather easily replaced sorts, such as *Philadelphus coronarius* or Barberry, as both of these are plants which stand abuse and shade. On the connecting wall, Pyracanthas should be trained, as well as Wisteria, and in the immediate corner between the south wall of the museum and the service-entrance gate, a little clump of Box may well be kept renewed. This is a space, also, where a few plants of *Leucothoe Catesbaei* and Japanese Holly (*Ilex crenata*) can be used and replaced when needed.

The door in the "tunnel" wall should have one accent-plant nearby, and here a good-sized evergreen, such as the box-leaved Japanese Holly (*Ilex crenata buxifolia*), or a second-rate Box (*Buxus sempervirens*) may be used.

At the kitchen-entrance steps *Spiraea Vanhouttei* has been used, as this endures abuse; but this particular variety of shrub is not insisted upon, as others, such as *thunbergii* or *trichocarpa*, would do equally well. All of this area should be carpeted with Ivy, Honeysuckle, and Violets, as it is both impossible and unwise to attempt to grow grass in these small and shaded places.

The service entrance (no longer extant), 1959. LA-GP-25-92, Garden Archives, Dumbarton Oaks, Trustees for Harvard University.

Planting at the service entrance (no longer extant), 1959. LA-GP-2-7, Garden Archives, Dumbarton Oaks, Trustees for Harvard University.

PLANT LIST: THE SERVICE ENTRANCE DRIVE

AT THE THIRTY-SECOND STREET GATE AND MIDWAY ON THE WALK

Quercus alba, White oak

ALONG THE SOUTH SIDE OF THE WALK AND ON THE LATTICE FENCE

Leucothoe catesbaei [*Leucothoe fontanesiana*], Drooping leucothoe
Deutzia scabra, Fuzzy deutzia

Ilex crenata, Japanese holly
Hedera sp., Ivy
Viola sp., Wild violet

ALONG THE NORTH SIDE OF THE WALK

Buxus sempervirens, Common box
Abelia grandiflora, Glossy abelia
Cotoneaster horizontalis, Rock cotoneaster
Pyracantha coccinea, Fire thorn

Wisteria sinensis, Chinese wisteria
Hedera sp., Ivy
Hedera helix, English ivy
Viola sp., Wild violet

AT THE STEPS TO THE RECEIVING ROOM

Philadelphus coronarius, Mock orange

AT THE DOOR IN THE EAST CORNER OF THE TUNNEL WALL

Ilex buxifolia [*Ilex crenata* 'Buxifolia'], Box-leaved Japanese holly

THE TUNNEL WALL AND CORNER

Hedera sp., Ivy
Ilex fujisanensis [*Ilex pedunculosa*]

Jasminum nudiflorum, Winter jasmine
Pyracantha coccinea, Fire thorn

BETWEEN THE KITCHEN ENTRANCE AND THE BASEMENT DOOR

Spiraea vanhouttei, Van Houtte spirea

PLANT LIST: THE STREET SIDE OF THE THIRTY-SECOND STREET WALL

FLANKING THE WEST ENTRANCE GATE AND THE
GARDEN GATE NORTH OF THE MUSEUM BUILDING

Buxus sempervirens, Common box

ESPALIERED ON THE WALLS OF THE MUSEUM BUILDING

Magnolia grandiflora, Southern magnolia

ON THE GARDEN WALLS

Ampelopsis lowii [*Parthenocissus
    tricuspidata* 'Lowii'], Boston ivy
Jasminum nudiflorum, Winter jasmine

Pyracantha coccinea 'Lalandei',
    Leland's fire thorn
Wisteria sinensis, Chinese wisteria

HANGING OVER THE WALL, FROM THE COPSE

Cedrus deodara, Deodar cedar
Tsuga canadensis, Canadian hemlock
Magnolia grandiflora, Southern magnolia
Acer platanoides, Norway maple
Acanthopanax pentaphyllus
    [*Acanthopanax sieboldianus*],
    Five-leaved aralia
Forsythia intermedia, Border forsythia

Ilex crenata, Japanese holly
Jasminum nudiflorum, Winter jasmine
Ligustrum vulgare, Common privet
Lonicera fragrantissima,
    Winter honeysuckle
Philadelphus coronarius, Mock orange
Spiraea prunifolia, Bridal Wreath

Inside the Thirty-Second Street Wall

The character of this landscape has changed since the construction of the Pre-Columbian Gallery in 1963, but its purpose remains to provide privacy and screening from the street. Due to the addition of the gallery, the space available for plantings has been reduced to a single row of American holly. These produce such deep shade that maintaining understory plantings has been a challenge. Plans are underway to thin the holly trees and to restore the understory planting using *Camellia* × 'Survivor'.   —JK

THE COUNSEL GIVEN FOR THE PROTECTION OF DUMBARTON OAKS FROM the surrounding streets applies to the various frontages. The area just inside the Thirty-second Street wall should be planted with taller plant material than parts of the R Street frontage. Between the driveways, or paths, and the wall, there should be an ample growth of deciduous trees, such as Oak or Tulip trees, which are long lived and will give high protection and screening from neighboring buildings during the summer season. The Oaks should, as generally recommended for the other parts of the place, be chosen almost entirely from the White Oak types, such as *Quercus alba* and *bicolor*; and it should be constantly kept in mind that the Oaks of peculiar and conspicuous growth, such as the Pin Oak (*Quercus palustris*), should be kept out as much as possible from the plantations. The small-leaved Oaks, such as the two mentioned, the laurel-leaved Oaks (*Quercus phellos*), and a few of the Black Oaks (*Quercus velutina*) will probably give a sufficient choice from which the plantations can be formed.

Under the "cover" of the tall deciduous trees, a heavy under-shrub plantation should be constantly maintained, mainly of evergreen material such as the American Holly (*Ilex opaca*), small Hemlocks which may be renewed from time to time as they deteriorate, and groups of superannuated Box bushes which are no longer in condition to use in the more conspicuous plantations. An occasional *Deodara* may be used, but it must be acknowledged that these are temporary trees and may need renewal every fifteen or twenty years. As these street screens are vitally important to the whole picture at Dumbarton, attention should be incessantly given to the feeding, watering, and cultivation of the street borders so that little loss and replacement will be needed.

Where the Thirty-second Street border plantations also mark the edge of the path, or road, the "facing down" material may be of deciduous or semi-evergreen plants. An occasional Forsythia in the sunny places, and, in the more shaded areas, white Azaleas, Japanese Holly (*Ilex crenata*), *Abelia grandiflora*, and possibly an occasional Yew, may be used to bolster up the taller plants closer to the wall and to hide the bare lower sections where these will in time appear in the border plantations.

The ground cover through this whole section should be mainly of English Ivy, but in order not to have the cover too monotonous, occasional patches of Periwinkle (*Vinca minor*) or Honeysuckle may be used. The warning is given that Honeysuckle, while a good ground cover is a troublesome one, as it soon invades shrubs and small trees, and, if neglected, may easily strangle them by its hard-twining stems and enveloping foliage.

It would be difficult to give a precise planting plan for any of these border plantations, as trees must be replaced when needed, but the choice of plant material should not be too wide a one, as border plantations are intended as screens and not as ornaments. Therefore, they should melt into the whole composition, rather than intrude themselves into an otherwise quiet scene.

PLANT LIST: THE THIRTY-SECOND STREET BORDER PLANTATION

Cedrus deodara, Deodar cedar
Picea excelsa [*Picea abies*], Norway spruce
Tsuga canadensis, Canadian hemlock
Ilex aquifolium, English holly
Ilex opaca, American holly
Magnolia grandiflora, Southern magnolia
Acer palmatum, Japanese maple
Acer platanoides, Norway maple
Cornus florida, Flowering dogwood
Koelreuteria paniculata, Varnish tree
Magnolia kobus, Kobus magnolia
Magnolia stellata, Star magnolia
Ostrya virginiana, Blue beech
Quercus alba, White oak
Quercus palustris, Pin oak
Quercus prinus, Chestnut oak
Quercus velutina, Black oak

Leucothoe catesbaei [*Leucothoe fontanesiana*], Drooping leucothoe
Ligustrum vulgare, Common privet
Pieris japonica, Japanese andromeda
Acanthopanax pentaphyllus [*Acanthopanax sieboldianus*], Five-leaved aralia
Azalea arborescens [*Rhododendron arborescens*], Sweet azalea
Celtis occidentalis, Hackberry
Elaeagnus pungens, Thorny eleagnus
Hibiscus syriacus, Rose-of-Sharon
Ligustrum amurense, Amur privet
Lonicera fragrantissima, Winter honeysuckle
Philadelphus coronarius, Mock orange

Plantings North of the Music Room

One of two large oaks still dominate the main bed that is planted with American holly, young white oak, and an understory of *Aucuba*, *Camellia*, and *Pieris* with accompanying ground cover. The smaller area that Farrand writes about was transformed into Ondine's Walk, named after the intricate brick walkway that seems to splash into the Copse-like waves breaking on the shore. This masterful brickwork was designed and installed in 2008 by longtime masonry contractor John Alden Pond Jr., who has been preserving and restoring the hardscaping at Dumbarton Oaks for over twenty-five years.   —JK

ON THE WALLS OF THE MUSIC ROOM ITSELF, WALL-TRAINED MAGNOLIA grandiflora have been used to mask the northeast and northwest corners. In between the arched windows, plants of Ivy have been trained, and, if they thrive,

Ondine's Walk leading north toward the Copse, 2007. Photograph by Gail Griffin.

The Pre-Columbian Gallery, looking north toward the remaining Copse. LA-GP-38-13, Garden Archives, Dumbarton Oaks, Trustees for Harvard University.

should be allowed to grow to the cornice, though not veiling the attractive proportions of this north face of the building.

In the little garden on the north side of the office, it has been thought essential to use evergreen material, but not of heavy or massive foliage as the enclosure is so small that large-leaved plants, such as Rhododendrons or Magnolias, would completely dwarf the small space. In this little enclosure, *Ilex crenata Fortunei* has been used as the main backbone of the planting, and as a support and relief to the *Pieris japonica* and the *Rhododendron mucronatum* (or *Azalea indica*) which constitute the main balance of the planting. On the walls dividing the office from the North Vista, and also from the Music Room, *Jasminum nudiflorum*, Ivy, and Honeysuckle are used, as it has been thought advisable to fluff over these walls in order to take away from the minute and almost cell-like quality of the little office garden. An occasional plant of *Parthenocissus quinquefolia Engelmannii* may be used on the east wall of the Music Room in order to lighten up the mass of Ivy, which might otherwise be too heavy and dark in its summer appearance. The ground carpet should be of *Vinca*. This small, office garden is also one of the few places where the southern *Prunus caroliniana* will live with any degree of happiness. It is not felt that this plant is essential to this position, but its lustrous evergreen leaves give a variety to the planting which might otherwise be lacking.

The Copse North of the Music Room

The character and size of this designed woodland has changed significantly since the construction of the Pre-Columbian Gallery in 1963, and its importance to the overall garden design has been reduced. One of the more important vantage points for this landscape is through the windows of the Pre-Columbian Gallery, that provide panoramic views of the garden. The objects displayed on translucent mounts seem to float in the forest, and this effect underscores the importance of maintaining a healthy evergreen understory.

—JK

THE IDEA BEHIND THE PLANTING IN THE COPSE IS TO KEEP IT AS POETIC and delicate in its appearance as possible; therefore, the early-spring flowers of the *Benzoin*, the floating flowers of the Dogwood, and slender shoots of the Japanese Maple are all used because of the delicacy of their effect. The copse should be the sort of place in which thrushes sing and in which dreams are dreamt.

The copse presents a difficult planting problem, as its west border immediately adjoins Thirty-second Street. Several houses on the west side of Thirty-second Street should be screened by evergreen plantations along the west side of the copse. The ideal trees to choose for this purpose are *Cedrus Deodara* and Hemlock. It is recognized, however, that severe winters may take a heavy death toll among the *Deodara* and that therefore the quantity used may have to be reduced to not more than four or five in the space between the north end of the new museum wing and the driveway to the greenhouse and service court. It is not thought wise to suggest using Pine trees in this neighborhood, as the Hemlock, with its fine foliage and its toleration of shade, is more likely to thrive than a sun-loving plant such as the White Pine.

The boundary planting along the street must be carefully watched and kept as thick as possible, and when the tall-growing plants become leggy, underplanting must be done, which may be chosen from *Pieris japonica* or *floribunda*, *Kalmia latifolia*, *Ilex Aquifolium* and *opaca*, *Leucothoe Catesbaei*, and such semi-evergreen material as *Lonicera fragrantissima*, *Elaeagnus pungens*, and *Ligustrum vulgare* and *ovalifolium*. Behind this west-boundary planting, tall high-branched Oaks should always make the bulk of the tree-planting of the copse, and the White Oak (*Quercus alba*) the Black Oak (*Quercus velutina*) and *Quercus prinus* are suggested. It will be

noted that no insistence is made on the use of *Quercus palustris*, the Pin Oak, or *Quercus rubra*, the Red Oak, as both of these are thought not particularly in harmony with the general character of the copse. The leaf size of the Red Oak is rather too large in scale to harmonize with the foliage of the White and bicolor, and the habit of growth of *palustris* is too drooping where a high-branched tree, such as *Quercus velutina* or *alba*, is necessary.

Behind the evergreen planting along Thirty-second Street, an occasional clump of Box (*Buxus sempervirens*), groups of the early-flowering Jasmines (*Jasminum nudiflorum*), and an occasional plant of Inkberry (*Ilex glabra*) may help to fill in, together with an occasional plant of Yew (*Taxus cuspidata* or *baccata*). Even a few *Magnolia grandiflora* may be used, to make a complete contrast with the fine foliage of the Hemlocks and *Deodara*.

Along with the other deciduous trees, one or two Hackberries (*Celtis occidentalis*) and a few Red Maples and several Beeches and one or two Elms are entirely proper to use. As for mid-height planting, the flowering Dogwood (*Cornus florida*) should be used in considerable quantity, as this seems to float in the air under the shadow of the big trees when it is in its blooming season. A few plants of *Philadelphus coronarius* near the Music-Room terrace give scent at the blooming season; and the foliage of *Acanthopanax pentaphyllus* is delicate and graceful, and its arching twigs are attractive, in this particular situation. There are also occasional groups of the Amur Privet (*Ligustrum amurense*), and a few Rose-of-Sharon (*Hibiscus syriacus*), and the Blue Beech (*Ostrya virginiana*) which does surprisingly well in this unlikely position. The use of the Norway Maple is discouraged, as the foliage of this tree is coarse and uninteresting in comparison with the Oaks, the Hackberries, the Elm, and the Red Maple; but one or two trees of Locust (*Robinia Pseudoacacia*) make a good contrast to the heavier foliage of the Oaks, and even a Varnish tree (*Koelreuteria paniculata*) or two add variety to what should never become a monotonous canopy of foliage.

Among the other mid-height plant material, there should always be a group of Spicebushes, (*Benzoin aestivale*) and *Magnolia stellate*, and on the east side of the copse two magnificent plants of *Magnolia Kobus* should be cherished and replaced, as their bloom is one of the loveliest of the spring features of the west boundary of the North Vista.

The green-leaved Japanese Maple (*Acer palmatum*) is also valuable to use for a mid-height plant; the delicacy of its foliage in the spring and summer adds distinct lightness and grace to the planting, and its autumn leaves add color to a somewhat colorless plantation. A few Azaleas, such as *Rhododendron arborescens* and the white *mucronatum* (*Azalea indica alba*), may be used for walk borders and

This eighteenth-century Provençal fountain was originally located in the Copse, shown here in 1930, before being relocated to the Ellipse following the construction of the Pre-Columbian Gallery. LA-GP-15-02, Garden Archives, Dumbarton Oaks, Trustees for Harvard University.

The Bowling Green, looking east, ca. 1948. LA-GP-7-6, Garden Archives, Dumbarton Oaks, Trustees for Harvard University.

The Bowling Green fountain, ca. 1948. LA-GP-7-13, Garden Archives, Dumbarton Oaks, Trustees for Harvard University.

where small material is desirable. The Black Cherry (*Prunus serotina*) is used there for its early flower. As it is much liked by birds, its disadvantage as a collector of caterpillars must be accepted.

A few plants of *Viburnum Carlesii* and *Burkwoodii*, set out near the terrace, will give spring and early-summer scent, but as the shade canopy is so heavy, the evergreen plants in the immediate neighborhood of the Music Room may have to be replaced frequently. It must be carefully borne in mind that while the copse must always be kept a distinct piece of forest, it must not be allowed to grow so rank and encumbered by its plantations that the distances are reduced by clumps of shrubs which hide the French fountain in the northwest part of the copse or which hide the lovely distances under the Oak branches looking north from the Music Room. The trees and shrubs must be kept so moderated in their growth that those sitting on the terrace north of the Music Room, or using the copse walks, should feel themselves in an open woodland rather than in a crowded shrubbery.

The ground carpet of the woodland should be as nearly as possible evergreen. *Lonicera japonica*, where used, must be kept controlled and mowed, as otherwise it will engulf all the shrubs, but it is useful for its scent and its semievergreen winter

PLANT LIST: THE COPSE NORTH OF THE MUSIC ROOM

TREES, SHRUBS, AND VINES

Cedrus deodara, Deodar cedar
Picea excelsa [*Picea abies*],
    Norway spruce
Pinus strobus, White pine
Tsuga canadensis, Canadian hemlock
Ilex opaca, American holly
Magnolia grandiflora, Southern magnolia
Acer palmatum, Japanese maple
Acer platanoides, Norway maple
Acer rubrum, Red maple
Fagus americana [*Fagus grandifolia*],
    American beech
Magnolia kobus, Kobus magnolia
Magnolia stellata, Star magnolia
Ostrya virginiana, Blue beech
Prunus serotina, Wild black cherry
Quercus alba, White oak
Quercus palustris, Pin oak
Quercus rubra, Red oak
Robinia pseudoacacia, Black locust
Ulmus americana, American elm
Ulmus fulva [*Ulmus rubra*], Slippery elm
Taxus gracilis [*Taxus baccata* 'Pendula'],
    English yew
Buxus sempervirens, Common box
Ilex buxifolia [*Ilex crenata* 'Buxifolia'], Box-
    leaved Japanese holly
Ilex crenata 'Fortunei' [*Ilex crenata*
    'Latifolia'], Japanese holly
Ilex crenata 'Macrophylla',
    Big-leaf Japanese holly
Kalmia latifolia, Mountain laurel

Leucothoe catesbaei [*Leucothoe*
    fontanesiana], Drooping leucothoe
Ligustrum amurense, Amur privet
Pieris floribunda, Mountain andromeda
Pieris japonica, Japanese andromeda
Prunus caroliniana, Cherry laurel
Rhododendron maximum, Rosebay
Abelia grandiflora, Glossy abelia
Acanthopanax pentaphyllus
    [*Acanthopanax sieboldianus*],
    Five-leaved aralia
Azalea arborescens [*Rhododendron*
    arborescens], Sweet azalea
Azalea indica [*Rhododendron indicum*],
    Macranthum azalea
Azalea indica alba [*Rhododendron*
    mucronatum], Snow azalea
Benzoin aestivale [*Lindera benzoin*],
    Spicebush
Forsythia suspensa, Weeping forsythia
Lonicera fragrantissima,
    Winter honeysuckle
Lonicera japonica, Japanese honeysuckle
Philadelphus coronarius, Mock orange
Pyracantha coccinea 'Lalandei',
    Leland's fire thorn
Viburnum burkwoodii,
    Burkwood viburnum
Ampelopsis quinquefolia [*Parthenocissus*
    quinquefolia], Woodbine
Hedera helix, English ivy

GROUND COVERS

Ampelopsis veitchii [*Parthenocissus*
    tricuspidata 'Veitchii'], Boston ivy
Convallaria majalis, Lily-of-the-valley
Hedera helix, English ivy
Lonicera sp., Honeysuckle

Pachysandra terminalis,
    Japanese pachysandra
Vinca minor, Periwinkle
Viola sp., Wild violet

Money plant, *Lunaria annua*. Photograph by Sandy Kavalier.

appearance. *Vinca*, Lily-of-the-valley, white Violets, and many spring bulbs should make the balance of the underplanting; but *Pachysandra* should be used only occasionally, as the foliage and growth of this plant has neither the elegance nor the color of the Vinca. The spring bulbs used should be the small ones, such as *Scilla siberica* and its white variety, and *Chionodoxa Luciliae* near the edges of the walks. And farther back, where higher plant material is suggested, the old-fashioned small *Leedsii* daffodils'[1] have a woodland quality which seems to make them entirely fitted for this place. Varieties such as Mrs. Langtry and White Lady are both inexpensive and attractive, and should be used generously. Also, groups of the English Bluebell (*Scilla nutans*),[2] in both its blue and white varieties, with perhaps an occasional group or two of *Scilla campanulata*,[3] the Spanish Bluebell, for later effect.

The planting of the east border of the copse has been spoken of as part of the frame for the west side of the North Vista, and the use of Hemlocks and Pines recommended.

No rigid rule is intended to be laid down for the planting of this area, as occasionally other sorts may be used, such as the Slippery Elm (*Ulmus fulva*); but it is suggested that certain types of trees be avoided, such as Ash, which remain leafless too late in the spring, and Walnut, as their growth is ungainly in comparison with the structure of the Oaks which should always be the mainstay in the planting of this forest canopy.

1 *Hortus* Third: *Narcissus incomparabilis*
2 *Hortus* Third: *Endymion nonscriptus*
3 *Hortus* Third: *Endymion hispanicus*

The Director's House and Terrace

The garden, Bowling Green, and house have become a hub of activity for staff and fellows, following the conversion of the house into the Refectory, where scholars, students, staff, and docents dine in a communal setting. One can gather on the Bowling Green, now clothed in pea gravel, and sit at any of the tables under the shade of a pair of original sycamore trees. The charming fountain with its rocaille walls and shelves add movement and sound to this popular space.   —JK

IT GOES WITHOUT SAYING THAT THE PLANTING AROUND THE DIRECTOR'S house must be attractive throughout the year, and as the winter months are those in which the house will be mainly used, the accent should be placed on evergreen material rather than on deciduous shrubs which might be dreary in winter.

The entrance-front of the house faces south, toward a hillside planted fairly heavily with deciduous trees which are valuable for their shade in summer; but high-growing Box or Japanese Holly should not be planted in front of the windows, which need all the winter southern light. At the east end of the house, outside the service windows, taller material may be planted, but not to such an extent as to keep the summer air out of the service wing. The lattice screen at the service door should be planted fairly thickly with Ivy, and possibly a few Honeysuckles; only a moderate amount of evergreen material, such as Box or Japanese Holly (*Ilex crenata*), is needed outside the trellis. The ground carpet of the hillside south of the front door should be a solid mass of Ivy (*Hedera helix*), kept within bounds and moderate in its height. It should be neatly trimmed around the brick platform and kept neatly trimmed on either side of the walks to the two south doors. A group or two of *Pachysandra* may be used near the service wing, and a few spring bulbs set out in the space between the house and the walk, if there is room in the carpet of Vinca, Violets, and Ivy. The Box bushes should be chosen of rather chubby types, not too tall, as tall plants would dwarf this pretty south facade.

The big Plane trees (*Platanus occidentalis*) seem well placed in the composition. On the west side of the house, separating it from the service road to the garage court, the Hemlocks on the roadside will probably need to be renewed when they become overgrown or shabby. There will be a constant need, as years pass, to renew the Hemlocks in the neighborhood of this house, west, south, and east.

Former director's residence, now the Refectory, ca. 1960. LA-GP-12-3, Garden Archives, Dumbarton Oaks, Trustees for Harvard University.

The upper part of the south hill is probably best kept in the present plantation of Rhododendron maximum, as these give good deep green in winter, are little trouble to take care of, and appear to thrive in this position. One or two Pine trees, overlooking the North Vista wall, are thought likely to be needed as a relief to an otherwise overdark green frame to the North Vista.

On the director's house itself, the Wisteria planted on its south side should be kept trained at the top of the first story and surrounding the little pediment at the south entrance. Occasional plants of Japanese Honeysuckle may be added, here and there, for scent; and toward the east end of the building, a few plants of Rose-of-Sharon (*Hibiscus syriacus*) and *Philadelphus coronarius* may be found attractive.

PLANT LIST: THE DIRECTOR'S HOUSE AND TERRACE

TREES, SHRUBS, AND VINES

Cedrus deodara, Deodar cedar

Pinus strobus, White pine

Tsuga canadensis, Canadian hemlock

Acer rubrum, Red maple

Acer saccharinum dasycarpum [*Acer saccharinum*], Silver maple

Ostrya virginiana, Blue beech

Platanus occidentalis, Buttonwood

Taxus gracilis [*Taxus baccata* 'Pendula'], English yew

Buxus sempervirens, Common box

Buxus sempervirens 'Suffruticosa', Edging box

Euonymus radicans [*Euonymus fortunei*], Winter creeper

Rhododendron maximum, Rosebay

Forsythia intermedia, Border forsythia

Hibiscus syriacus, Althaea

Ligustrum amurense, Amur privet

Lonicera japonica, Japanese honeysuckle

Philadelphus coronarius, Mock orange

Spiraea prunifolia, Bridal Wreath

Ampelopsis quinquefolia [*Parthenocissus quinquefolia*], Woodbine

Ampelopsis veitchii [*Parthenocissus tricuspidata* 'Veitchii'], Boston ivy

Lycium halimifolium, Common matrimony vine

Wisteria sinensis, Chinese wisteria

GROUND COVERS

Hedera helix, English ivy

Pachysandra terminalis, Japanese pachysandra

Vinca minor, Periwinkle

Viola sp., Wild violet

The Service Driveway from
Thirty-Second Street to the Garage Court

The screening effect desired by Farrand is now mainly accomplished by a series of Japanese maples, their sinuous branches complimenting the winding drive and adding to the sense of mystery as one descends. Few hemlocks remain, and the understory contains primarily aucuba, camellia, and winter jasmine. Study is underway to restore the eastern bed along the drive, as the exposure here is more open and the hemlock and aucuba are no longer thriving.   —JK

AS THE DROP IN THE LEVEL BETWEEN THE FOOT OF THIRTY-SECOND STREET and the garage court, beside the greenhouse, is a very considerable one, the road is steep, and therefore more difficult to deal with from the point of view of design than if it had been possible to make a less tortuous and precipitous driveway. The space between the buildings is limited, and as the road is constantly used it must be kept screened from both the superintendent's cottage on the west and the director's house on the east. The main planting on either side of this road should be a fairly frequently renewed series of Hemlocks (*Tsuga canadensis*), as this is a plant of delicate foliage and yet evergreen. At the base of these Hemlocks, where needed, small groups of Mountain Laurel (*Kalmia latifolia*) may be planted, in order to make the Hemlock planting less monotonous than if continuous. This is also true of the Japanese Maple (*Acer palmatum*), of which a few may be used. One or two *Deodaras* (*Cedrus Deodara*) should also be used, as the place is sheltered and the trees are likely to thrive; but it is not thought desirable to continue the planting of *Catalpa*, Norway Maple (*Acer platanoides*), *Spiraea*, or Silver Maple (*Acer saccharinum*). The big Tulip tree (*Liriodendron tulipifera*) standing south of the coolhouse is a magnificent specimen, and should be preserved as long as it is safe to retain it and as long as it can be kept in reasonably good condition. When it must go, it should not be replaced, as the coolhouse does not require this extra deciduous shade on the south, and the planting of smaller evergreens will be sufficient as a screen to the northeast side of the superintendent's cottage.

Ground cover of Ivy and Vinca may be used freely on both sides of the road and up to both houses.

The road surrounds a grass plat in the asymmetrical court. As the space could not be fitted into a balanced design, any planting on the grass plat will look

crooked from some points of view. Therefore, it is recommended that, when possible, the good Beech tree (*Fagus sylvatica cuprea*) now growing in the middle of this space, which was moved in more-or-less accidentally, be placed somewhere in the neighborhood of the Rose Garden, where it will fit into the composition more smoothly than in its present position.

On the north front of the garage, the planting should be kept almost entirely to wall-trained Wisteria and Ivy. This is equally true of the south sides of the potting shed and greenhouse, as it is important that the court be kept unencumbered, since it is used for summer-plant storage and should not have its space reduced by planting.

On the wall and trellis on the east side of the court, many creepers may be grown which will add a feature of interest—wall-trained *Forsythia*, Ivy, possibly a Bittersweet or two, perhaps a *Clematis* or two if they will stand the hot western sun in summer.

The service drive, looking up the sinous path toward 32nd Street, 2021.
Photograph by Sandy Kavalier.

The Garage Court

Along with the Bowling Green, the Garage Court has also become a hub of activity, following the library construction in 2005. A constant stream of staff and fellows flow in and out of the library, and gardeners utilize the court for plant staging and garden access, as this path into the garden is the only one large enough for equipment to pass into the lower gardens. The greenhouse, designed by renowned architects McKim, Mead & White, is still used to propagate and grow annuals, vegetables, and perennials, as well as to house the orchid and tropical plant collections that are displayed throughout the campus.

—JK

THE NORTH SIDE OF THE GARAGE SHOULD HAVE WALL-TRAINED *WISTERIA sinensis* of the purple variety. This creeper should be kept to single-stem plants, and should be trained in prim, horizontal lines, which will emphasize the story heights, window spaces, and, on the corners, the outline of the building. An under-planting of Ivy is desirable in order to give some warmth of color to these walls.

At the foot of the building, one or two Box plants of the tree sort may be used; and on the oil-pump house a further planting of Wisteria and Ivy.

On the east side of the garage it is desirable to keep the big Sycamore (*Platanus occidentalis*), as in both spring and winter they are interesting, in flower, young foliage, or bark.

The Copper Beech (*Fagus sylvatica cuprea*) in the center of the court should be removed when possible, and not replaced, as it is not possible to plant a tree in this peculiarly shaped lawn without its being off-center either of greenhouse or coolhouse.

On the south wall of the greenhouse, Ivy should be planted to hide the lower walls, and Wisteria on the porch grill. Box markers are desirable on either side of the greenhouse and coolhouse entrances.

On the west side of the garage, Ivy and yellow Jasmines may be planted, and on the south walls, more Ivy and more Jasmines.

The planting on the south side of the garage should be kept low enough so that it does not interfere with the light in the windows of the living quarters. There should, however, be an effective screen at the east end of the garage where the

The Garage Court and greenhouses, featuring Farrand's signature kidney-shaped bed, 1932. LA-GP-23-11, Garden Archives, Dumbarton Oaks, Trustees for Harvard University.

service windows are placed; possibly a lattice screen covered with Ivy and *Clematis* would be more effective than free-standing planting.

If it is possible to maintain in good condition a low Box border on the south side of the greenhouse and on the north side of the garage, this border can enclose little working-beds south of the greenhouse, and small, flower or bulb-beds north of the garage.

It is thought not desirable to use deciduous shrubs in the garage court; therefore when the *Spiraea*, *Weigela*, and *Philadelphus* have perished, they need not be renewed.

The Superintendent's Cottage

The landscape has been altered here to serve its current purpose as an operations center for Dumbarton Oaks. The elm trees have not been kept inside the wall, in order to ensure adequate light indoors, and the beds outside the walls have been transformed into annual display beds, with a backdrop of *Nandina* and roses rambling along the top of the wall. *Buxus sempervirens* 'Suffruticosa', *Pyracantha*, wisteria, and *Philadelphus* are still grown around the house foundation in a nod to Farrand's plant palette. —JK

ON THE SOUTH OF THE HOUSE, BETWEEN THE COTTAGE AND THE STREET, a pair of American Elms had probably always better be maintained, as they frame the gable and the south facade of the house attractively from the street aspect, and from the house itself screen the street opposite. Between the street wall and the house, formerly a small lawn was planted, but the shade of the trees now makes this impossible, and the space had therefore eventually better be flagged or graveled for use in summer. The reason for planting deciduous trees, rather than evergreens, in this position is that the shade is needed in the summer only, and if evergreens should be substituted for deciduous trees the house would be unduly dark in winter.

On the north side of the brick wall, a hedge of *Pyracantha* should be kept slightly below the top of the iron fence, as, if allowed to grow too high it dwarfs the facade of the house as seen from the street. Some sort of evergreen hedge should be kept in this position, if it be found necessary later to replace the *Pyracantha*.

On the house itself, wall-trained *Wisteria sinensis* should be kept subdued and in architectural harmony with the building facade. Ivy and *Pyracantha* also are planted on the building walls and are valuable for their winter effect. On the east side of the house, between it and the road leading to the garage, a few evergreens such as *Kalmia*, Box, and *Ligustrum japonicum* may be used as a screen and to give additional privacy to the south and east fronts of the house. It is hoped that the indiscriminate planting of mixed shrubs around the house can be discouraged, as it is thought that the building will gain attractiveness by simplified, rather than elaborated, groups—a few flowering Dogwood, possibly one or two English Thorn (*Crataegus monogyna*, formerly known as *oxycantha*). North and east of the house, a few *Exochorda racemosa* may be used, a few more flowering Dogwoods

The Superintendent's Cottage now services the Dumbarton Oaks Operations department, 2021. Photograph by Sandy Kavalier.

PLANT LIST: THE SUPERINTENDENT'S COTTAGE

TREES, SHRUBS, AND VINES

Pinus strobus, White pine
Tsuga canadensis, Canadian hemlock
Acer palmatum, Japanese maple
Celtis occidentalis, Hackberry
Cornus florida, Flowering dogwood
Crataegus monogyna, English hawthorn
Liriodendron tulipifera, Tulip poplar
Morus rubra, American mulberry
Ulmus americana, American elm
Buxus sempervirens, Common box
Kalmia latifolia, Mountain laurel
Ligustrum japonicum, Wax-leaf privet
Rhododendron maximum, Rosebay

Cydonia japonica [*Chaenomeles japonica*],
    Japanese quince
Exochorda racemosa, Pearl bush
Forsythia intermedia, Border forsythia
Kolkwitzia amabilis, Beautybush
Lagerstroemia indica, Crape myrtle
Philadelphus coronarius, Mock orange
Pyracantha coccinea 'Lalandei',
    Leland's fire thorn
Hedera sp., Ivy
Lonicera japonica, Japanese honeysuckle
Wisteria sinensis, Chinese wisteria

GROUND COVER, PERENNIALS AND SPRING BULBS

Chrysanthemum sp., Chrysanthemum
Scilla sp., Squill

Tulipa sp., Tulip
Vinca minor, Periwinkle

(*Cornus florida*), and perhaps a Crape Myrtle (*Lagerstroemia indica*), but the *Spireas*, Elders, and other temporary shrubs should be used in very small measure.

The ground cover may be of Ivy and, where possible, *Vinca*. In the spring, a few bulbs, such as a few groups of Tulips, on the south side of the house, make the surroundings look friendly and attractive; and perhaps standard Fuchsias in summer may be set in the same bulb borders, to be replaced in the late autumn with a few groups of Chrysanthemums. But no effort should be made to keep a continuous flowering border, as the shade and the heat on the south side of this house make it an almost impossible task to keep flowers, or even ground cover, in good condition.

On the north side of the house are a few deciduous trees, such as the Tulip tree (*Liriodendron tulipifera*) and Japanese Maple (*Acer palmatum*); and if those living in the cottage are interested in birds, a Mulberry tree, such as *Morus indica*,[4] will attract birds, although the Mulberry is not a particularly tidy tree for the neighborhood of a house.

4   *Hortus* Third: *Morus australis*

The Knoll to the West of the Superintendent's Cottage

This area, now known as the "Dell," provides an excellent view to the passerby on S Street through the elegant iron fence with acorn finials. A curving path designed by Jim Urban in the mid-2000s follows the contours of the slope as it leads to the library. An excellent example of a mature beech, oak, and hemlock climax community, the Dell is carefully managed to prevent encroachment by invasive plants. Many of Farrand's plant selections will no longer thrive in the deep shade of the mature trees, but native plants such as Rhododendron and Lindera add interest while keeping the understory relatively open.

—JK

IT HAS BEEN FELT FOR SOME TIME THAT THE WIRE FENCE ON S STREET should someday be replaced by a brick wall, somewhat in the character of the wall on the south side of the Superintendent's cottage but without its iron cresting, and of sufficient height to make a distinct deterrent to the casual curiosity of passersby. While the present wire fence remains, it should be kept well covered with Japanese Honeysuckle.

On the hilltop is a magnificent group of American Beeches, mixed with a few Silver and Red Maples. Norway Maples (*Acer platanoides*) should not be tolerated in this group of fine natural trees, but eventually more Tulip trees (*Liriodendron*) may be set out, as they make a pleasant, slight shade above the Rhododendron planting in the dell between the Superintendent's cottage and the knoll.

On the walk leading to the Superintendent's cottage, and between the groups of Rhododendrons, there is room for an occasional Dogwood (*Cornus*) or Spicebush (*Benzoin aestivale*).[5] The shrubs lying north of the knoll should be a continuation of those set out specifically for cutting purposes for the buildings, and should be chosen from the varieties that are of most use for this purpose. For example, the American Snowball (*Viburnum trilobum*), the English Snowball (*Viburnum Opulus*), the *Deutzia* (both *gracilis* and *scabra*) and the various Spireas (*Thunbergii*, *prunifolia*), the Japanese Snowball (*Viburnum tomentosum plicatum*)[6]

5 *Hortus* Third: *Lindera Benzoin*
6 *Hortus* Third: *Viburnum, plicatum tomentosum*

and the old-fashioned Syringa and its new French hybrids, will give ample cutting material for the buildings during the flowering season. The lower part of this knoll has been used as the hospital for invalid plants, but these should be removed to some other place as soon as the ground which they now cover is needed for some permanent purpose.

PLANT LIST: THE KNOLL TO THE WEST OF THE SUPERINTENDENT'S COTTAGE

Tsuga canadensis, Canadian hemlock
Acer rubrum, Red maple
Acer saccharinum, Silver maple
Fagus grandifolia, American beech
Gleditsia triacanthos, Honey locust
Hicoria [*Carya*] sp., Hickory
Liriodendron tulipifera, Tulip poplar
Morus alba, White mulberry
Morus rubra, American mulberry
Platanus occidentalis, Buttonwood
Prunus serotina, Wild black cherry
Robinia pseudoacacia, Black locust
Sassafras sp., Sassafras
Taxus baccata, English yew
Buxus sempervirens, Common box
Buddleia sp., Butterfly bush

Chionanthus virginicus, Fringe tree
Deutzia gracilis, Slender deutzia
Forsythia intermedia, Border forsythia
Kolkwitzia amabilis, Beautybush
Rhus sp., Sumac
Spiraea thunbergii, Thunberg spirea
Viburnum opulus,
      European cranberry bush
Vitex heterophylla [*Vitex negundo heterophylla*], Chaste tree
Jasminum nudiflorum, Winter jasmine
Lonicera japonica, Japanese honeysuckle
Lycium halimifolium,
      Common matrimony vine
Narcissus sp., Daffodil

The Cottage Northeast of the Fellows' Quarters

The character of this cottage (now known as Acorn Cottage) in the woods remains intact, though the trees have matured and light levels have decreased. Following Farrand's suggestion for simplicity and minimum upkeep, this area is managed as an extension of the Dell. The patio, steps, and walls were restored in 2021.   —JK

THE LITTLE COTTAGE LYING ON THE HILLSIDE NORTHEAST OF THE fellows' quarters is surrounded and protected by trees: Hemlocks on the east and west, with a few Box bushes near the cottage itself. The forest growth comes fairly close to the cottage, and consists of a Silver Maple (*Acer saccharinum*), the Red Maple (*Acer rubrum*), the Tulip tree (*Liriodendron tulipifera*), the native Hickory, the Black Walnut (*Juglans nigra*), the Locust (*Robinia Pseudoacacia*), the wild Cherry (*Prunus serotina*), American Elm (*Ulmus americana*), and American Beech (*Fagus ferruginea*).

On the south slope of the hill, Crabapples, wild Plum and Cherry, a few Ash trees, and Box Elder make up most of the woodside, under-planted with the big Rhododendron (*Rhododendron maximum*) and carpeted on the edges with *Pachysandra*, Ivy, and Violets. The planting surrounding this hedge should be kept as simple as possible so as to minimize upkeep, as the position is a remote one and should not entail any minute upkeep such as is needed for flower beds or carefully trained creepers. Therefore, it is suggested that Woodbine (*Parthenocissus quinquefolia*) and Ivy be the plants used on the house, and that flowers, if needed, should be from *Narcissus* or other hardy bulbs, Rhododendrons, and Dogwood.

The path to the Northeast cottage from the service walk is bordered with flowering shrubs, which have been planted in this position in order to be available for cut flowers for the quarters and the main building. Therefore, the Japanese Quince (*Chaenomeles japonica*) should be maintained, as long as it is possible to keep it free from scale, as should the common and Persian and white Persian Lilac, the Beautyberry (*Callicarpa purpurea*), *Abelia grandiflora*, *Hibiscus syriacus*, and Witch hazel (*Hamamelis virginiana*). The neighborhood of this walk has been used as a sort of hospital for ailing plants, and this hospital-nursery may be kept here as long as the ground is not required for another purpose. An occasional plant of some evergreen material, such as Box or Yew, would add a touch of green in the winter, and, if thought advisable, a few clumps of the hardy *Narcissus* or the sturdiest *Iris* could be put among the roots of the shrubs.

The path from the fellows' quarters to the cottage is bordered by trees and should be kept shady but not allowed to become elaborately planted in any way which requires much upkeep. The same forest border as is spoken of in the planting east of the northeast cottage, should edge the east side of this path. This wood border now consists of the Silver Maple, Honey Locust, Locust, and Wild Cherry, with an occasional sprout of *Paulownia* which should not be encouraged, as the leaf is far too big in scale for the forest surroundings.

Under the forest trees, Dogwood, Rhododendron, Spicebush, Sassafras, and Mountain Laurel would be wise to maintain as forest border, with an occasional group of Rhododendrons or *Kalmia* which seem to be detached and yet a part of the main, Rhododendron hillside planting. Simplicity should be emphasized in this planting, and minimum upkeep.

PLANT LIST: THE COTTAGE NORTHEAST OF THE FELLOWS' QUARTERS

TREES, SHRUBS, AND VINES

Tsuga canadensis, Canadian hemlock
Ilex opaca, American holly
Acer negundo, Box elder
Acer platanoides, Norway maple
Acer rubrum, Red maple
Acer saccharinum, Silver maple
Cercis canadensis, Redbud
Fagus ferruginea grandifolia
    [*Fagus grandifolia*], American beech
Fraxinus sp., Ash
Gleditsia triacanthos, Honey locust
Hicoria [*Carya*] sp., Hickory
Juglans nigra, Black walnut

Liriodendron tulipifera, Tulip poplar
Malus sp., Crabapple
Morus rubra, American mulberry
Prunus americana, Wild plum
Prunus serotina, Wild black cherry
Robinia pseudoacacia, Black locust
Ulmus americana, American elm
Buxus sempervirens, Common box
Rhododendron sp., Rhodendron
Rhododendron maximum, Rosebay
Benzoin aestivale [*Lindera benzoin*],
    Spicebush

GROUND COVERS, PERENNIALS, AND SPRING BULBS

Hedera sp., Ivy
Narcissus sp., Daffodil
Pachysandra sp., Pachysandra

Tulipa sp., Tulip
Vinca minor, Periwinkle
Viola sp., Wild violet

PLANT LIST: THE PATH BETWEEN THE SERVICE WALK
AND THE COTTAGE NORTHEAST OF THE FELLOWS' QUARTERS

TREES, SHRUBS, AND VINES

Acer rubrum, Red maple

Liriodendron tulipifera, Tulip poplar

Prunus serotina, Wild black cherry

Ulmus americana, American elm

Taxus hibernica [*Taxus baccata* 'Stricta'], Irish yew

Rhododendron sp., Rhododendron

Abelia grandiflora, Glossy abelia

Callicarpa purpurea [*Callicarpa dichotoma*], Chinese beautyberry

Chaenomeles japonica, Japanese quince

Hamamelis virginiana, American witch hazel

Hibiscus syriacus, Rose-of-Sharon

Lonicera japonica, Japanese honeysuckle

Philadelphus coronarius, Mock orange

Syringa persica, Persian lilac

Syringa persica 'Alba', White Persian lilac

Syringa vulgaris, Common lilac

PERENNIALS AND SPRING BULBS

Iris sp., Flag

Narcissus sp., Daffodil

Tulipa sp., Tulip

PLANT LIST: THE AREA BETWEEN THE FELLOWS' HOUSE
AND THE COTTAGE TO ITS NORTHEAST

TREES, SHRUBS, AND VINES

Tsuga canadensis, Canadian hemlock

Acer platanoides, Norway maple

Acer saccharinum, Silver maple

Ailanthus glandulosa [*Ailanthus altissima*], Tree-of-heaven

Cornus sp., Dogwood

Fagus ferruginea grandifolia [*Fagus grandifolia*], American beech

Gleditsia triacanthos, Honey locust

Hicoria [*Carya*] sp., Hickory

Juglans nigra, Black walnut

Liriodendron tulipifera, Tulip poplar

Morus alba, White mulberry

Morus rubra, American mulberry

Paulownia tomentosa, Karri tree

Platanus occidentalis, Buttonwood

Prunus serotina, Wild black cherry

Robinia pseudoacacia, Black locust

Sassafras sp., Sassafras

Ulmus americana, American elm

Buxus sempervirens, Common box

Kalmia latifolia, Mountain laurel

Rhododendron sp., Rhododendron

Benzoin aestivale [*Lindera benzoin*], Spicebush

Forsythia sp., Forsythia

GROUND COVERS AND SPRING BULBS

Lonicera sp., Honeysuckle

Narcissus sp., Daffodil

Vinca minor, Periwinkle

Viola sp., Wild violet

The Fellows' Quarters

The landscape in front of the building has been maintained true to Farrand's vision. The wisteria specimen that drapes the façade in purple blooms has been meticulously trained and is beautiful year-round. A mixture of dogwoods of varying species informally clusters around the west end of the space, along with an ancient crabapple tree, likely from Farrand's original planting, that still produces gorgeous, atypically large apples.

—JK

THE SOUTH FRONT OF THE FELLOWS' QUARTERS IS DIVIDED INTO THREE units, the main building making the north face of the small courtyard and containing the assembly rooms. The entrance courtyard is graveled, as it was originally built so that the cars of the workmen who used to occupy this building could be properly kept from the public street. If, in time, the graveled court is no longer thought necessary for the fellows' quarters, it might be changed into a lawn bisected by a flagged walk to the main door, but the planting probably should remain as simple as it was planned, since the upkeep around this building should be minimized. On the south wall of the main building, purple and white Wisteria should be trained, together with Ivy (*Hedera helix*) and the winter-blooming Jasmine (*Jasminum nudiflorum*). The building will be occupied mainly in winter, therefore emphasis should be placed more on evergreen than deciduous material. This makes the importance of winter-flowering Jasmine and of Ivy obvious.

The walk leading in from S Street, through a little garden space to the east entrance to the fellows' quarters, has a grass plat on its west side in which a *Magnolia grandiflora* is planted. Here, against the south face of the house, a *Pyracantha coccinea* should be kept carefully trimmed and from overspreading the building. On the building walls, further planting of Ivy, Wisteria, and Jasmine should clothe the wall without smothering it. It is important that this little enclosure be made attractive and be kept simple and not overplanted. One or two shrubs, such as the early-summer-flowering *Viburnum Carlesii*, the bright-colored *Berberis Thunbergii*, or the early-summer-flowering *Philadelphus coronarius*, will in all likelihood be sufficient. Against the fence to the south, if any planting be needed, a hedge of *Pyracantha* may be kept closely trimmed and

The immaculately trained wisteria clinging to the front of the Fellows' Quarters (now the Guest House) is a showstopper in the spring and is visible from the public sidewalk on S Street, 2021. Photograph by Sandy Kavalier.

PLANT LIST: THE FELLOWS' QUARTERS

THE CENTRAL ENTRANCE AND EAST APARTMENT COURTYARD

Magnolia grandiflora, Southern magnolia
Cornus florida, Flowering dogwood
Ligustrum japonicum, Wax-leaf privet
Abelia grandiflora, Glossy abelia
Berberis thunbergii, Japanese barberry
Elaeagnus sp., Eleagnus
Philadelphus coronarius, Mock orange
Pyracantha coccinea, Fire thorn
Rosa 'Mermaid', Mermaid rose
Rosa 'Silver moon', Silver moon rose
Spiraea prunifolia, Bridal Wreath
Spiraea thunbergii,
    Thunberg spirea

Viburnum carlesii,
    Mayflower viburnum
Clematis jackmanii,
    Jackman clematis
Jasminum nudiflorum,
    Winter jasmine
Wisteria sinensis 'Alba',
    White Chinese wisteria
Wisteria sinensis 'Purpurea',
    Purple Chinese wisteria
Hedera sp., Ivy
Iris sp., Flag
Viola sp., Wild violet

THE WEST APARTMENT COURTYARD

Magnolia grandiflora, Southern magnolia
Cornus florida, Flowering dogwood
Ligustrum japonicum, Wax-leaf privet
Berberis thunbergii, Japanese barberry
Elaeagnus sp., Eleagnus
Jasminum nudiflorum, Winter jasmine
Pyracantha coccinea, Fire thorn

Rosa 'Mlle. Cécile Brunner',
    Cécile Brunner rose
Alcea sp., Hollyhock
Aquilegia sp., Columbine
Hedera helix, English ivy
Iris sp., Flag
Tulipa sp., Tulip

THE STEPS FROM THE WEST APARTMENT TO THE SERVICE DRIVE

Abelia grandiflora, Glossy abelia
Deutzia gracilis, Slender deutzia
Philadelphus coronarius, Mock orange
Spiraea prunifolia, Bridal Wreath
Viburnum plicatum, Japanese snowball

Viburnum tomentosum
    [*Viburnum plicatum tomentosum*],
    Doublefile viburnum
Alcea sp., Hollyhock

---

not higher than the fence. There may be places in this little enclosure where the Silver Moon or Mermaid Rose could be used; and, unquestionably, the carpet under the fence of Violets, Ivy, and Iris would be attractive both in winter and summer. The *Pyracantha* hedge was trained into an arch over the walk, but it is thought likely that this will eventually be eliminated, as when last seen it appeared rather heavy in scale to be appropriate as an adjunct to so small a building.

THE BORDER (EXAMPLES ONLY)

Alcea sp., Hollyhock
Aquilegia sp., Columbine

Iris sp., Flag
Tulipa sp., Tulip

WEST OF THE DRIVEWAY

Malus sp., Apple (Delicious, Duchess, Early red, Williams, Winesap)

Pyrus sp., Pear (Golden seckle, Grimes, Transcendent)
Vitus sp., Grapevine

THE SERVICE DRIVE

Cornus mas, Cornelian cherry
Salix vitellina [*Salix alba vitellina*], Golden willow
Callicarpa purpurea [*Callicarpa dichotoma*], Chinese beautyberry
Chaenomeles japonica, Japanese quince
Exochorda racemosa, Pearl bush

Hydrangea grandiflora [*Hydrangea paniculata* 'Grandiflora'], Peegee hydrangea
Pyracantha coccinea 'Lalandei', Leland's fire thorn
Clematis jackmanii, Jackman clematis

THE BORDER OF THE SERVICE DRIVE

Nandina domestica, Heavenly bamboo
Aquilegia sp., Columbine
Chrysanthemum sp., Chrysanthemum (Korean hybrid)

Salvia sp., Sage
Scabiosa sp., Scabious
Teucrium sp., Germander
Verbena sp., Vervain

AT THE IMMEDIATE REAR OF THE BUILDING

Abelia grandiflora, Glossy abelia
Rosa sp., Rose
Spiraea prunifolia, Bridal Wreath
Spiraea thunbergii, Thunberg spirea
Syringa vulgaris, Common lilac
Weigela sp., Weigela

Alcea sp., Hollyhock
Baptista tinctoria, Wild indigo
Deutzia gracilis, Slender deutzia
Monarda sp., Wild bergamot
Salvia sp., Sage
Scabiosa sp., Scabious

At the west entrance to the fellows' quarters, two *Magnolia grandiflora* should balance the planting at the east entrance to this building, and Dogwood as well. The hedge of *Pyracantha* also should balance the hedge at the east end of the building, and it is equally true that the west-entrance arch will probably have to be simplified and reduced to an appropriate size. If it is possible to maintain a border around the lawn of each of these enclosures of Hollyhock, Columbine, Iris, and Tulips it is desirable to do so, but not essential, as the upkeep of the principal gardens may absorb all the attention it is possible to give to the plantations of the institution. The planting on the wall of the west side of the quarters should approximately correspond to the planting on the east wing: the Ivy and Jasmine should be repeated, a climbing Rose or two, and, possibly, one or two flowering shrubs. It will be easy to overplant these two entrances, and difficult to make them simple.

Japanese wisteria,
Wisteria floribunda.
Photograph by
Sandy Kavalier.

The Enclosed Yard to the North of the Fellows' Quarters

With its current configuration of residence above and operational space below, the north yard of the Guest House now serves support services. On the east end of the yard, a majestic American beech marks the end of the Dell, and a small nursery has been created west of this in which boxwood and other essential plants are propagated and grown. West of the nursery, hardscaping provides a useful work surface and staging area. North of this yard sits Gardeners' Court, the south front of which has been decorated with many of Farrand's favorite plants, including wisteria grown on a horizontal support across the building face. —JK

WHEN THE FELLOWS' QUARTERS WAS FIRST BUILT, IT WAS USED AS A carpenter shop and property garage. Since it has been altered to living quarters for the resident fellows, the work yard, which was appropriate in connection with the machine shop and carpenter shop, becomes less and less appropriate as a near neighbor. It is hoped that in time the yard may be very considerably reduced in size; and, if this be the case, the fence surrounding it should be carefully salvaged, as it is made of British rift-oak paling and should last for many a year, even in the Washington climate. If the present yard could be reduced to half its size, the whole southern end might be planted to evergreens and deciduous shrubs, which would conceal the northern half of the yard. It is thought that the smaller yard would probably be sufficiently large to serve the smaller grounds which are now the home grounds of Dumbarton Oaks.

The trees surrounding the yard ought to be mainly evergreen, such as White Pine [*Pinus Strobus*], Norway Spruce [*Picea Abies*], and Hemlock; and against this evergreen plantation a few single Cherries, Dogwoods, and Camellias would be attractive, to give spring flower and autumn berry.

In the neighborhood of the quarters, some sort of small nursery would be desirable, for either invalid plants or small material of future use to the Dumbarton gardens.

Construction of the Fellows' Quarters and north yard, 1934. LA-GP-16-1, Garden Archives, Dumbarton Oaks, Trustees for Harvard University.

PLANT LIST: THE AREA TO THE NORTH OF THE FELLOWS' QUARTERS

THE ENCLOSED YARD WEST OF THE PROPERTY YARD

Magnolia grandiflora, Southern magnolia
Acer saccharinum, Silver maple
Malus sp., Apple
Prunus armeniaca, Apricot
Prunus serotina, Wild black cherry

Prunus 'Windsor', Windsor cherry
Robinia pseudoacacia, Black locust
Ligustrum japonicum, Wax-leaf privet
Hibiscus syriacus, Rose-of-Sharon

NORTH OF THE ENCLOSED YARD

Magnolia grandiflora, Southern magnolia
Acer rubrum, Red maple
Acer saccharinum, Silver maple
Hicoria [*Carya*] sp., Hickory
Castanea dentata, American chestnut
Juglans nigra, Black walnut
Morus rubra, American mulberry
Robinia pseudoacacia, Black locust
Salix vitellina [*Salix alba vitellina*],
 Golden willow
Ulmus americana, American elm
Taxus baccata, English yew

Buxus sempervirens, Common box
Rhododendron sp., Azalea
Cydonia vulgaris [*Cydonia oblonga*],
 Common quince
Ficus sp., Fig
Forsythia sp., Forsythia
Syringa vulgaris, Common lilac
Jasminum nudiflorum, Winter jasmine
Rosa sp., Shrub rose
Rosa multiflora, Baby rose

IN THE BORDER

Alcea sp., Hollyhock
Iris sp., Flag

Tulipa sp., Tulip